Life can be a bit crazy, right? Well, what if I told you there's an ancient guide that can help you deal with all the ups and downs in a super practical way? Welcome to "Stoic 75 Rules: A Guide to a Better Life." In this book, we're diving into something called Stoicism. It's not just a bunch of old ideas; it's like a toolkit for handling the everyday stuff, from the good moments to the tough ones. You've got these 75 rules to help you out, and we're going to make them easy to understand and actually use in your life.

Stoicism is all about taking charge of how you react to things, understanding what really matters, and finding your way through challenges. Each rule here isn't just a saying; it's like a little story that helps you get what it's all about. Plus, we're giving you practical tips so you can put these ideas into action. So, whether you're new to this Stoicism thing or you've heard about it before, these rules are like your friendly guides to making life better. They'll help you handle problems, appreciate the good stuff, and find more meaning in your day-to-day.

This book is like a friend offering you some cool advice to make your life more awesome. Ready to dive in? Let's get started on this journey to a better, wiser, and happier you!

Table of Contents

1) Focus on What You Can Control
2) You Control How You Respond to Things
3) Ask Yourself, "Is This Essential?"
4) Meditate on Your Mortality Every Day
5) Value Time More Than Money/Possessions
6) You Are the Product of Your Habits
7) Remember You Have the Power to Have No Opinion
8) Own the Morning
9) Put Yourself up for Review (Interrogate Yourself)
10) Don't Suffer Imagined Troubles
11) Try to See the Good in People
12) Never Be Overheard Complaining…Even to Yourself
13) Two Ears, One Mouth…For a Reason (Zeno)
14) There Is Always Something You Can Do
15) Don't Compare Yourself to Others
16) Live as if You've Died and Come Back (Every Minute Is Bonus Time)
17) "The Best Revenge Is Not to Be Like That." Marcus Aurelius
18) Be Strict with Yourself and Tolerant with Others
19) Put Every Impression, Emotion, to the Test Before Acting on It
20) Learn Something from Everyone
21) Focus on Process, Not Outcomes
22) Define What Success Means to You
23) Find a Way to Love Everything That Happens (Amor Fati)
24) Seek Out Challenges
25) Don't Follow the Mob
26) Grab the "Smooth Handle"
27) Every Person Is an Opportunity for Kindness (Seneca)
28) Say No (A Lot)
29) Don't Be Afraid to Ask for Help
30) Find One Thing That Makes You Wiser Every Day
31) What's Bad for the Hive Is Bad for the Bee (Marcus Aurelius)
32) Don't Judge Other People

33) Study the Lives of the Greats
34) Forgive, Forgive, Forgive
35) Make a Little Progress Each Day
36) Journal
37) Prepare for Life's Inevitable Setbacks (Premeditatio Malorum):
38) Look for the Poetry in Ordinary Things
39) To Do Wrong to One Is to Do Wrong to Yourself (Sympatheia)
40) Always Choose "Alive Time"
41) Associate Only with People That Make You Better
42) If Someone Offends You, Realize You Are Complicit in Taking Offense
43) Fate Behaves as She Pleases…Do Not Forget This
44) Possessions Are Yours Only in Trust
45) Don't Make Your Problems Worse by Bemoaning Them
46) Accept Success Without Arrogance, Handle Failure with Indifference
47) Courage. Temperance. Justice. Wisdom. (Always)
48) The Obstacle Is the Way
49) Ego Is the Enemy
50) Stillness Is the Key
51) Don't Let the Past Control Your Present
52) Understand the Power of Your Thoughts
53) Embrace Change as a Constant
54) Speak Less, Listen More
55) Cultivate Resilience in the Face of Adversity
56) Choose Quality Over Quantity in Relationships
57) Practice Gratitude Daily
58) Find Joy in the Journey, Not Just the Destination
59) Master the Art of Letting Go
60) Balance Ambition With Contentment
61) Be Mindful of Your Inner Dialogue
62) Cherish Moments of Solitude
63) Practice Humility in Success
64) Learn to Differentiate Between Wants and Needs

65) Strive for Inner Harmony
66) Express Love and Appreciation
67) Let Your Actions Speak Louder Than Your Words
68) Value Inner Wealth Over External Validation
69) Foster a Growth Mindset
70) Practice Random Acts of Kindness
71) Celebrate Others' Success Without Envy
72) Invest in Lifelong Learning
73) Balance Rest and Productivity
74) Cultivate a Sense of Wonder
75) Practice Mindful Consumption

1) Focus on What You Can Control:

Anecdote: Picture a ship navigating stormy seas. The captain cannot control the weather, but they can control the ship's course.

Interpretation: Stoicism emphasizes the power lies in our reactions. By directing energy only towards what we control, we foster resilience and inner peace. Direct your energy towards things within your control, like your actions and reactions.

Practical Tool: Create a "Circle of Control" list. Identify what is within your control and consciously redirect energy from the rest. Before reacting, ask, "Can I control this?" If not, let it go.

The practical involves creating a "Circle of Control" list to identify what is within your control and consciously redirecting energy away from what is not. It emphasizes the importance of asking whether you can control a situation before reacting and encourages letting go of things beyond your control.

Create a "Circle of Control" List:

This tool starts with the creation of a list that categorizes aspects of your life into two circles - one for things within your control and another for things outside your control.

1. Within Your Control: List aspects of your life that you have direct influence over, such as your actions, reactions, thoughts, and decisions.

2. Outside Your Control: Identify elements that are beyond your control, such as external events, other people's behaviors, or outcomes that are not solely determined by your actions.

Consciously Redirect Energy: Once you have identified what is within and outside your control, the focus is on consciously redirecting your energy.

This involves acknowledging that you have limited resources and choosing to invest your time and efforts where they can make a positive impact.

Before Reacting, Ask "Can I Control This?":

Before reacting emotionally to a situation, pause and ask yourself whether the issue at hand is within your control. This moment of reflection allows you to make a conscious decision about how to respond.

1. If Yes:
    - If the situation is within your control, you can choose a proactive response. Take deliberate actions to address or improve the situation.

2. If No:
    - If the situation is beyond your control, the tool encourages letting it go. Accept that you cannot control everything and choose not to invest unnecessary energy in things that won't lead to positive outcomes.

How to Implement the Tool:

1. Identify Elements: Take time to identify elements in your life that fall within and outside your control. This could be done through reflection or journaling.

2. Create the Circles: Physically or metaphorically create the circles. This could involve writing down the aspects in each circle or visualizing them.

3. Consciously Redirect Energy: When faced with a challenge or situation, remind yourself to focus on what you can control. Redirect your energy towards proactive and constructive actions.

4. Ask the Question: Before reacting emotionally, pause and ask yourself, "Can I control this?" This simple question serves as a checkpoint for conscious decision-making.
5. Letting Go: Practice letting go of situations that are outside your control. This does not mean apathy but a conscious choice not to be consumed by things beyond your influence.

Benefits of the "Circle of Control" Tool:

1. Reduced Stress: By focusing on what's within your control, you can reduce stress associated with trying to control the uncontrollable.
2. Improved Decision-Making: Making decisions based on what you can control leads to more effective and strategic choices.
3. Enhanced Emotional Well-being: Letting go of things beyond your control contributes to emotional well-being and resilience.
4. Increased Productivity: Redirecting energy towards actionable items improves productivity and efficiency.
5. Better Relationships: Understanding and respecting the boundaries of control can lead to healthier relationships by avoiding unnecessary conflicts.

This tool is a practical strategy for managing stress and enhancing emotional well-being by focusing on what can be controlled and consciously letting go of what cannot. It encourages a more intentional and mindful approach to navigating life's challenges. Again, by identifying what you can control, you empower yourself to make positive changes where it matters. The key is to consciously choose where to direct your energy, focusing on the actionable aspects of your life and letting go of the things that are beyond your influence. This practice promotes a sense of inner calm and resilience in the face of uncertainties.

2) You Control How You Respond to Things:

Anecdote: Imagine a traffic jam. You cannot control the traffic, but you can control how you react to the situation.

Interpretation: Our reactions define us. Choosing a composed response in challenging situations is a mark of virtue. Your power lies in your response, not external events.

Practical Tool: Practice responding, not reacting. Pause, reflect, and then choose your response consciously. Take a breath before reacting. Choose a response that aligns with your values.

The practical tool is focused on cultivating mindfulness and intentional communication.

Practice Responding, Not Reacting: This tool emphasizes the importance of being mindful and intentional in your responses to various situations, conversations, or challenges. Instead of reacting impulsively based on emotions or immediate impulses, the emphasis is on taking a more thoughtful and measured approach.

Steps to Implement the Tool:

1. Pause and Reflect:
    - When faced with a situation that triggers an emotional response, take a moment to pause.
    - Give yourself time to reflect on your emotions, thoughts, and the context of the situation.

2. Conscious Choice:
    - Instead of allowing emotions to dictate your response, make a conscious choice about how you want to respond.

- Consider the potential impact of different responses and choose one that aligns with your values and long-term goals.

3. Take a Breath:
    - Physically taking a breath can serve as a powerful metaphorical and physiological cue to slow down.
    - Breathing helps to calm the nervous system, providing you with the mental space to make a more considered choice.

4. Alignment with Values:
    - Ensure that your chosen response aligns with your personal values and principles.
    - Consider how your response reflects your character and contributes to positive communication and relationships.

Benefits of Practicing Response Over Reaction:

1. Reduced Conflict: By responding thoughtfully, you are less likely to escalate conflicts unnecessarily.

2. Improved Relationships: Thoughtful responses contribute to healthier communication patterns, fostering positive relationships.

3. Enhanced Emotional Intelligence: Practicing this tool enhances emotional intelligence by developing self-awareness and self-regulation.

4. Personal Growth: Making conscious choices in responses leads to personal growth as you learn to navigate challenges with intentionality.

5. Effective Communication: Thoughtful responses contribute to more effective and meaningful communication.

Overall, the tool encourages individuals to be proactive in their communication style, fostering a more positive and constructive approach to various situations.

3) Ask Yourself, "Is This Essential?":

Anecdote: Consider a cluttered closet. Is each item essential or just adding chaos?

Interpretation: Prioritize essentials to avoid being consumed by trivial matters, fostering a mindful existence. Prioritize what truly matters to avoid unnecessary stress.

Practical Tool: Implement a daily reflection on your actions. Ask, "Is this essential to my values or just a distraction?" Regularly evaluate tasks and possessions, keeping only what adds value.

The practical tool focuses on daily reflection and intentional living by regularly assessing actions, tasks, and possessions against personal values.

Implement a Daily Reflection on Your Actions: This tool encourages individuals to engage in a daily practice of self-reflection to assess the alignment of their actions with their values. The aim is to cultivate mindfulness and purposeful living.

Steps to Implement the Tool:

1. Daily Evaluation:
    - Set aside time each day for a brief reflection on your actions, decisions, and experiences.
    - Consider the events of the day and your responses to them.
2. Questioning:
    - Ask yourself whether the actions you took were essential to your values or if they were merely distractions.
    - Consider whether your choices are aligned with your long-term goals and principles.

3. Task and Possession Evaluation:
    - Extend this reflection to your tasks and possessions.
    - Evaluate whether your daily tasks contribute to your overall objectives or if they are distractions.
    - Assess possessions and consider whether they add value to your life or if they are unnecessary.
4. Value-Based Decision Making:
    - Use your values as a guiding framework for decision-making.
    - When faced with choices, evaluate them based on whether they resonate with your core values.
5. Simplify and Prioritize:
    - Regularly assess your tasks and possessions, prioritizing those that align with your values.
    - Simplify your life by eliminating unnecessary tasks and possessions that do not contribute to your well-being.

Benefits of Daily Reflection:

1. Clarity of Purpose: Regular reflection provides clarity on what is truly important to you, reinforcing your sense of purpose.
2. Reduced Distractions: By distinguishing between essential activities and distractions, you can minimize time and energy spent on unproductive pursuits.
3. Increased Productivity: Focusing on tasks aligned with your values enhances productivity and goal achievement.
4. Enhanced Well-being: Eliminating non-essential tasks and possessions contributes to a simpler, more fulfilling life.

5. Mindful Living: Daily reflection fosters a mindful approach to life, encouraging intentional choices and actions.
6. Improved Decision-Making: Value-based decision-making leads to more informed and aligned choices.

This tool is a practical way to integrate mindfulness into daily living, ensuring that actions and possessions are in harmony with one's values and contributing to a more meaningful and intentional life.

4) Meditate on Your Mortality Every Day:

Anecdote: Picture an hourglass. Time is limited, and reflecting on mortality helps appreciate each moment.

Interpretation: Acknowledging mortality enhances appreciation for life, motivating purposeful living. Embrace the impermanence of life for a fuller appreciation of the present.

Practical Tool: Dedicate a few minutes daily for silent reflection on the transient nature of life. Set aside a few minutes daily to contemplate the brevity of life.

The practical tool involves dedicating a few minutes each day for silent reflection on the transient and fleeting nature of life.

Dedicate Daily Time for Silent Reflection: This tool encourages individuals to take a few moments each day to engage in silent reflection, contemplating the impermanence and brevity of life. The goal is to foster mindfulness, gratitude, and a deeper appreciation for the present moment.

Steps to Implement the Tool:

1. Designate a Quiet Space: Choose a quiet and comfortable space where you can be alone and undisturbed for a few minutes.

2. Set a Daily Time: Schedule a specific time each day for this silent reflection. It could be in the morning, before bedtime, or any time that suits your routine.
3. Silent Contemplation:
   - Sit or lie down comfortably and close your eyes.
   - Allow your mind to settle and focus on your breath to bring yourself into the present moment.
4. Reflect on Transience: During this silent time, contemplate the transient nature of life. Consider the fleeting moments and the impermanence of all things.
5. Gratitude Practice: Use this time to express gratitude for the present moment, acknowledging the preciousness of life.
6. Awareness of the Present: Bring your awareness to the current moment, appreciating the sights, sounds, and sensations around you.
7. Letting Go: Practice letting go of attachments to the past or worries about the future. Embrace the present moment fully.

Benefits of Daily Silent Reflection:

1. Mindfulness and Presence: Regular silent reflection enhances mindfulness, bringing a heightened awareness to the present moment.
2. Gratitude Cultivation: Contemplating the brevity of life fosters a sense of gratitude for the experiences and relationships in the present.
3. Stress Reduction: Taking moments for silent reflection can reduce stress by promoting relaxation and a sense of calm.
4. Perspective Shift: Reflecting on the transient nature of life can lead to a shift in perspective, prioritizing what truly matters.

5. Increased Emotional Resilience: Embracing the impermanence of life can contribute to emotional resilience, helping individuals navigate challenges with greater ease.
6. Enhanced Well-being: Incorporating silent reflection into daily life can contribute to overall well-being by fostering a deeper connection with the present and a greater appreciation for life.

This tool serves as a daily ritual for cultivating mindfulness, gratitude, and a profound awareness of the transient nature of our existence, encouraging individuals to live more fully in each precious moment.

5) Value Time More Than Money/Possessions:

Anecdote: Imagine trading a priceless antique for more time with loved ones.

Interpretation: Prioritize time for meaningful pursuits over material possessions, fostering a rich inner life. Time is irreplaceable; use it wisely.

Practical Tool: Create a time-budget, allocating hours to activities aligning with your values. Prioritize time for meaningful activities over accumulating possessions.

The practical tool involves creating a time-budget to allocate hours to activities that align with personal values. It emphasizes prioritizing meaningful activities over the accumulation of possessions.

Create a Time-Budget: This tool is about treating time as a valuable resource and intentionally allocating it to activities that reflect and align with your core values. It involves a conscious effort to prioritize how you spend your time.

Steps to Implement the Tool:

1. Identify Core Values: Start by identifying your core values. These could include aspects like relationships, personal growth, health, community, or career.

2. List Meaningful Activities: Make a list of activities that resonate with your values. These could be activities that bring you joy, contribute to your well-being, or align with your long-term goals.

3. Allocate Time: Create a time-budget by allocating specific hours to the identified meaningful activities. Consider daily, weekly, and monthly time allocations.

4. Prioritize Over Possessions: Emphasize the importance of allocating time to meaningful activities over the accumulation of possessions. This shift in focus encourages experiences and relationships over material possessions.

5. Regularly Review and Adjust:
   - Regularly review your time-budget to ensure that you are staying true to your values.
   - Be open to adjusting the allocation based on changing priorities or circumstances.

6. Set Boundaries: Establish boundaries to protect your time for meaningful activities. This may involve saying 'no' to activities that do not align with your values or learning to delegate tasks that don't contribute significantly to your well-being.

Benefits of Creating a Time-Budget:

1. Intentional Living: Allocating time based on values promotes intentional living, ensuring that your daily activities align with your broader life goals.
2. Enhanced Well-being: Prioritizing meaningful activities contributes to overall well-being by focusing on experiences and relationships that bring fulfillment.
3. Reduced Stress: A time-budget can help manage stress by allowing for a more balanced and purposeful distribution of time.
4. Clarity of Priorities: Creating a time-budget provides clarity on your priorities, helping you make decisions that align with your values.
5. Mindful Consumption:
    - By emphasizing experiences over possessions, this tool encourages mindful consumption and a more minimalist approach to life.
6. Improved Work-Life Balance: Allocating time intentionally can contribute to a healthier work-life balance, ensuring that personal and professional aspects of life are given due consideration.

This tool is a practical approach to time management that shifts the focus from mere productivity to purposeful living. It encourages individuals to prioritize activities that bring long-term satisfaction and align with their values, fostering a more fulfilling and meaningful life.

6) You Are the Product of Your Habits:

Anecdote: Envision a sculptor shaping clay. Your habits mold who you become.

Interpretation: Aristotle said, "We are what we repeatedly do." Habits shape character. Cultivate virtuous habits to become the best version of yourself. Consistent habits determine your character.

Practical Tool: Identify a positive habit, start small, and consistently integrate it into your routine. Cultivate positive habits consciously, as they shape your identity.

The practical tool involves the intentional cultivation of positive habits by identifying a small, positive behavior and consistently integrating it into your routine. It underscores the idea that these habits play a crucial role in shaping your identity.

Identify a Positive Habit: This tool starts with the identification of a positive habit that you want to incorporate into your daily life. Positive habits can vary widely, ranging from health-related behaviors to habits that enhance productivity, well-being, or personal growth.

Start Small: Rather than overwhelming yourself with drastic changes, the emphasis here is on starting small. Choose a manageable and achievable aspect of the positive habit to initiate. This makes it more likely that you will be able to integrate the habit into your routine successfully.

Consistently Integrate into Your Routine: Consistency is key when it comes to habit formation. Make a conscious effort to integrate the chosen positive habit into your daily or weekly routine. Set a specific time or trigger for the habit to increase the likelihood of it becoming a regular part of your life.

Cultivate Positive Habits Consciously: Approach the cultivation of positive habits with conscious awareness. Be mindful of the habit-building process and its impact on your overall well-being. Acknowledge the positive changes it brings to your life and recognize the efforts you are making to shape your identity positively.

How to Implement the Tool:

1. Choose a Positive Habit: Identify a positive habit that aligns with your goals and values. It could be something like daily exercise, practicing gratitude, reading regularly, or maintaining a healthy sleep routine.
2. Break it Down: Break down the habit into smaller, manageable components. For example, if your goal is to exercise daily, start with a 10-minute workout and gradually increase the duration.
3. Set a Trigger: Associate the habit with a specific trigger or existing routine. This helps in creating a natural integration into your day.
4. Track Progress: Keep a record of your progress. This could be in the form of a habit tracker, journal, or app. Regularly reviewing your progress reinforces the habit.
5. Adjust and Expand: As the habit becomes more ingrained, consider expanding or adjusting it to further align with your goals.

Benefits of Cultivating Positive Habits:

1. Identity Formation: Positive habits contribute to the formation of a positive identity, shaping how you perceive yourself and how others see you.
2. Improved Well-being: Habits that prioritize health, mindfulness, or personal growth can significantly enhance overall well-being.
3. Increased Productivity: Productive habits contribute to increased efficiency and effectiveness in various aspects of life.

4. Stress Reduction: Positive habits, especially those related to relaxation and self-care, can help reduce stress levels.
5. Long-term Impact: Cultivating positive habits consistently over time can have a lasting impact on your life trajectory and personal development.

This tool is a practical approach to personal development, emphasizing the power of small, positive changes in shaping your identity and enhancing the quality of your life.

7) Remember You Have the Power to Have No Opinion:

Anecdote: Think of a heated debate. You can choose not to engage.

Interpretation: Not every situation demands your opinion. Cultivate equanimity by choosing when to speak.

Practical Tool: Practice silence. In conversations, observe more and speak less, especially on trivial matters. Learn to step back and observe without feeling compelled to express a viewpoint.

The practical tool involves the intentional practice of silence, especially in conversations. It encourages individuals to observe more and speak less, particularly on trivial matters. The tool emphasizes the importance of stepping back, observing without immediately expressing a viewpoint, and fostering a mindful approach to communication.

Practice Silence in Conversations:

This tool is centered around the intentional choice to incorporate moments of silence into conversations. Rather than feeling compelled to fill every pause with words, it encourages individuals to embrace the power of silence for observation and reflection.

Steps to Implement the Tool:

1. Observe More, Speak Less: Cultivate a habit of observing more and speaking less, especially in situations where there is a tendency to contribute trivial or unnecessary information.

2. Mindful Listening: Actively engage in mindful listening. Instead of formulating your response while the other person is speaking, focus on truly understanding their perspective.

3. Step Back: Learn to step back mentally and emotionally in conversations. This involves resisting the urge to immediately share your viewpoint, allowing for a more thoughtful response.

4. Observe Without Compulsion: Practice observing without feeling compelled to express every thought or opinion. Allow thoughts to come and go without the need to verbalize them immediately.

5. Choose Meaningful Contributions: When you do speak, aim for contributions that are meaningful, relevant, and add value to the conversation. Avoid unnecessary chatter.

Benefits of Practicing Silence:

1. Enhanced Understanding: Actively listening and observing without immediately responding can lead to a deeper understanding of others' perspectives.

2. Improved Communication Quality: By speaking less and choosing more carefully when to express opinions, the overall quality of communication can improve.

3. Mindful Presence: Embracing moments of silence promotes mindful presence in conversations, allowing for a more genuine and thoughtful exchange.

4. Reduced Misunderstandings: Taking the time to observe before speaking can reduce the likelihood of misunderstandings and misinterpretations.
5. Respectful Communication: Practicing silence reflects a respectful communication style, valuing both your own thoughts and the contributions of others.
6. Cultivation of Patience: Learning to step back and observe without immediately responding fosters patience, promoting a more measured and thoughtful communication style.

How to Incorporate Silence:

1. Pause Before Responding: Intentionally pause before responding to allow for thoughtful consideration.
2. Practice Active Listening: Focus on what the other person is saying rather than formulating your response. This promotes a deeper level of engagement.
3. Limit Trivial Conversations: Be mindful of engaging in trivial conversations that may not contribute meaningfully to the interaction.
4. Mindful Breathing: If you find it challenging to remain silent, practice mindful breathing to center yourself before responding.
5. Reflect on Silence: Take time to reflect on the benefits of silence in your communication and observe any positive changes in your interactions.

This tool serves as a practical approach to fostering more mindful and intentional communication. By incorporating intentional moments of silence, individuals can create space for deeper understanding, meaningful contributions, and a more respectful exchange of ideas.

8) Own the Morning:

Anecdote: Picture a sunrise. The morning sets the tone for the day.

Interpretation: Start the day intentionally. Morning rituals enhance focus and set a positive trajectory. Start your day with purpose and positivity.

Practical Tool: Craft a morning routine that includes reflection, gratitude, and planning. Establish a morning routine that aligns with your goals.

The practical tool involves crafting a morning routine that incorporates reflection, gratitude, and planning. The goal is to establish a morning routine that aligns with your overarching goals and sets a positive tone for the day.

Craft a Morning Routine: This tool emphasizes the importance of starting your day with a purposeful and intentional routine. By incorporating elements of reflection, gratitude, and planning, you set the stage for a positive and productive day.

Components of the Morning Routine:

1. Reflection: Allocate time in your morning routine for reflection. This can involve thinking about your goals, values, and the intentions you have for the day.

2. Gratitude Practice: Cultivate a habit of expressing gratitude. This could be through journaling, mentally listing things you are thankful for, or incorporating gratitude affirmations.

3. Planning: Set aside time to plan your day. This includes identifying key tasks, priorities, and goals. Use this time to create a roadmap for the day ahead.

How to Implement the Tool:

1. Design Your Routine: Tailor your morning routine to your preferences and schedule. Consider the time you have available and how each component fits into your morning.

2. Start with Reflection: Begin your morning routine with a period of reflection. This could involve mindfulness exercises, meditation, or simply sitting quietly to collect your thoughts.

3. Express Gratitude: Dedicate a few minutes to expressing gratitude. This could be through writing in a gratitude journal or mentally acknowledging the positive aspects of your life.

4. Plan Your Day: Outline your day by identifying priorities and tasks. Consider both short-term and long-term goals and be realistic about what you can accomplish.

5. Consistency is Key: Strive for consistency in your morning routine. Establishing a routine helps signal to your brain that it is time to transition into a focused and intentional mindset.

Benefits of a Morning Routine:

1. Positive Mindset: Starting the day with reflection and gratitude promotes a positive mindset, setting the tone for a more optimistic day.

2. Increased Productivity: Planning your day in the morning allows you to prioritize tasks and set goals, contributing to increased productivity.

3. Stress Reduction: A well-structured morning routine can help reduce stress by providing a sense of control and organization.
4. Alignment with Goals: Crafting a morning routine that aligns with your goals ensures that your daily actions contribute to your overarching objectives.
5. Mindful Start: A morning routine fosters a mindful start to the day, promoting awareness and intentionality in your actions.
6. Establishing Habits: Consistently following a morning routine helps establish positive habits, reinforcing healthy and productive behaviors.

Adapt to Your Preferences:

1. Personalize Your Routine: Customize your morning routine based on what resonates with you. It could include activities like reading, exercise, or creative pursuits.
2. Be Flexible: While consistency is important, be flexible and adjust your routine based on changing circumstances. The key is to maintain the core components that align with your goals.

This tool serves as a practical guide to kickstarting your day with purpose and intention. By incorporating reflection, gratitude, and planning into your morning routine, you create a positive foundation for the rest of the day, fostering productivity, mindfulness, and alignment with your overarching goals.

9) Put Yourself up for Review (Interrogate Yourself):

Anecdote: Imagine a self-check-in like a performance review.

Interpretation: Regular self-reflection cultivates self-awareness, leading to continuous personal growth. Regularly assess your actions and decisions.

Practical Tool: Keep a nightly journal. Reflect on actions, emotions, and areas for improvement. Reflect on your day or week, identifying areas for improvement.

The practical tool involves keeping a nightly journal for reflection on actions, emotions, and areas for improvement. It emphasizes the importance of regularly reviewing and analyzing your day or week to identify areas where you can grow and make positive changes.

Keep a Nightly Journal: This tool encourages individuals to maintain a nightly journal as a dedicated space for reflection. The journal becomes a personal record of thoughts, emotions, and insights gained from the day.

Components of Nightly Journal Reflection:

1. Actions: Reflect on the actions you took during the day. Consider both positive and negative actions and their impact on yourself and others.

2. Emotions: Explore and document your emotional experiences throughout the day. Identify moments of joy, frustration, stress, or any other emotions that stood out.

3. Areas for Improvement: Deliberately focus on areas where you feel there is room for improvement. This could be related to

personal habits, communication, time management, or any other aspect of your life.

How to Implement the Tool:

1. Establish a Routine: Set a specific time each night to journal. This could be before bedtime or at the end of your workday. Consistency is key.

2. Reflect on Actions: Begin your journal entry by reflecting on the actions you took throughout the day. Consider both major and minor actions and their consequences.

3. Explore Emotions: Express your emotional experiences. Write about the highs and lows, as well as any patterns or triggers you observe in your emotions.

4. Identify Areas for Improvement: Dedicate a section of your journal to areas where you believe you could improve. This could involve personal development goals, behavioral changes, or specific actions you want to work on.

5. Set Realistic Goals: Based on your reflections, set realistic and achievable goals for improvement. These goals can serve as a roadmap for personal growth.

6. Celebrate Successes: Acknowledge and celebrate any achievements or positive aspects of your day. This reinforces a positive mindset.

Benefits of Keeping a Nightly Journal:

1. Increased Self-Awareness: Regular reflection promotes self-awareness by encouraging you to pay attention to your actions, emotions, and areas for improvement.

2. Goal Setting and Progress Tracking: Setting improvement goals and regularly reviewing them in your journal allows you to track your progress over time.
3. Stress Reduction: Journaling provides an outlet for processing emotions and can contribute to stress reduction.
4. Enhanced Decision-Making: Reflecting on your actions helps you make more informed decisions by learning from past experiences.
5. Positive Habit Formation: Keeping a nightly journal can become a positive habit that supports continuous personal growth and development.

Adapt to Your Preferences:

1. Choose Your Journal Format: Select a journal format that suits your preferences, whether it is a physical notebook, a digital journaling app, or another medium.
2. Experiment with Prompts: Experiment with journaling prompts to guide your reflections. Some prompts may focus on gratitude, specific achievements, or challenges faced during the day.
3. Include Positive Affirmations: Integrate positive affirmations into your journaling routine to reinforce a positive mindset.
4. Share Insights with Others: Consider sharing insights from your journal with trusted friends, family, or mentors. External perspectives can offer valuable insights.

This tool serves as a practical and adaptable method for continuous self-improvement. Keeping a nightly journal provides a structured space for reflection and goal setting, fostering personal growth and awareness.

10) Don't Suffer Imagined Troubles:

Anecdote: Visualize a shadowy forest. Fear of the unknown can be more daunting than reality.

Interpretation: Worrying about future troubles only burdens the present. Focus on solving actual challenges. Address actual problems instead of dwelling on imagined ones.

Practical Tool: When anxious, evaluate if the concern is real or imagined. Channel energy into addressing real issues. When anxious, assess if the concern is real or imagined before reacting.

The practical tool involves a two-step process when facing anxiety: evaluating whether the concern is real or imagined and channeling energy into addressing real issues. It emphasizes the importance of distinguishing between genuine problems and unfounded worries and encourages a measured response to anxiety.

Two-Step Approach to Anxiety:

1. Evaluate Real vs. Imagined Concerns: The first step involves a careful assessment of the nature of the anxiety. Determine whether the concern causing anxiety is based on a real, tangible issue or if it is an imagined fear without a concrete basis.

2. Channel Energy into Addressing Real Issues: If the concern is identified as real and tangible, the next step is to channel your energy into addressing the actual problem. Focus on practical steps and solutions rather than being consumed by anxiety.

How to Implement the Tool:

1. Pause and Reflect: When anxiety arises, take a moment to pause and reflect on the nature of the concern. Ask yourself whether it is a real, tangible issue or if it is an imagined fear.

2. Assess Realism: Consider the evidence or facts supporting the anxiety. Is there concrete evidence that the concern is valid, or is it based on assumptions, speculation, or irrational fears?

3. Differentiate Real and Imagined: Distinguish between concerns that have a tangible basis in reality and those that are more rooted in imagination or irrational fears.

4. Focus on Real Issues: If the concern is identified as real, shift your focus to addressing the actual problem. Identify practical steps and solutions that can be taken to resolve or mitigate the issue.

5. Mindful Response: Respond to real issues with a mindful and measured approach. Avoid reacting impulsively or letting anxiety dictate your actions.

Benefits of the Real vs. Imagined Assessment:

1. Reduced Stress: By differentiating between real and imagined concerns, you can reduce unnecessary stress caused by unfounded worries.

2. Effective Problem-Solving: Focusing on real issues allows for more effective problem-solving, as energy is directed towards practical solutions.

3. Improved Decision-Making: Assessing the realism of concerns helps in making more informed and rational decisions, especially in situations causing anxiety.

4. Enhanced Emotional Well-being: Addressing real issues contributes to improved emotional well-being, as it involves taking positive and constructive actions.
5. Avoidance of Unnecessary Anxiety: By consciously evaluating concerns, you can avoid being overwhelmed by anxiety triggered by imagined fears.

Adapt to Your Preferences:

1. Mindfulness Practices: Incorporate mindfulness practices, such as deep breathing or meditation, into the evaluation process to maintain a calm and focused mindset.
2. Journaling: Consider keeping a journal to document and assess your concerns. Writing down thoughts and feelings can provide clarity.
3. Seeking Support: If uncertain about the nature of the concern, seek support from friends, family, or a mental health professional to gain external perspectives.
4. Positive Affirmations: Integrate positive affirmations to reinforce a constructive mindset and counteract negative thoughts associated with imagined fears.

This tool provides a practical framework for managing anxiety by encouraging a thoughtful evaluation of concerns and a targeted response to real issues. By adopting this approach, individuals can navigate anxiety more effectively and focus their energy on constructive actions.

11) Try to See the Good in People:

Anecdote: Picture a rough diamond. Everyone has strengths; sometimes, they just need polishing.

Interpretation: Seeing good in others fosters empathy, reducing conflict and promoting harmonious relationships. Look for the positive qualities in others.

Practical Tool: When frustrated with someone, actively seek positive qualities in them, fostering compassion. Focus on understanding people's motivations and finding common ground.

The practical tool involves a two-step process when feeling frustrated with someone: actively seeking positive qualities in them to foster compassion and focusing on understanding their motivations while finding common ground. This tool promotes empathy and constructive communication, aiming to transform frustration into a more positive and compassionate mindset.

Two-Step Approach to Frustration:

1. Actively Seek Positive Qualities: When feeling frustrated with someone, deliberately shift your focus towards identifying positive qualities in that person. Look for aspects of their character, actions, or strengths that can evoke compassion.
2. Focus on Understanding and Finding Common Ground: Once you've acknowledged positive qualities, move on to understanding the motivations behind the person's actions. Seek common ground that can facilitate empathy and constructive communication.

How to Implement the Tool:

1. Recognize Frustration: Acknowledge when you are feeling frustrated with someone. This awareness is the first step towards implementing the tool.
2. Shift Focus to Positivity: Actively redirect your focus from the frustrating aspects to positive qualities in the person. Consider their strengths, kindness, or any positive actions that you have observed.
3. Empathize and Understand Motivations: Take a moment to empathize with the person by trying to understand their motivations. Consider their perspective, background, and the factors that might be influencing their behavior.
4. Find Common Ground: Identify common ground or shared values that can serve as a foundation for understanding. This could be a mutual goal, shared interests, or a common purpose.
5. Communicate Constructively: Approach the person with a mindset of understanding and empathy. Communicate your feelings and concerns in a constructive manner, emphasizing collaboration and finding solutions.

Benefits of the Positive Qualities and Understanding Approach:

1. Enhanced Compassion: Actively seeking positive qualities fosters compassion, helping you view the person in a more positive light.
2. Improved Communication: Focusing on understanding motivations and finding common ground promotes constructive communication, fostering a more collaborative approach.
3. Conflict Resolution: By seeking common ground, you create a basis for resolving conflicts and finding solutions that are acceptable to all parties involved.

4. Reduced Negative Emotions: Shifting focus to positive qualities and understanding motivations can help reduce negative emotions associated with frustration.
5. Strengthened Relationships: The tool contributes to building stronger relationships by promoting empathy, understanding, and open communication.

Adapt to Your Preferences:

1. Mindfulness Practices: Incorporate mindfulness practices, such as deep breathing or meditation, to center yourself before actively seeking positive qualities.
2. Gratitude Journaling: Keep a gratitude journal where you document positive qualities in people. This habit reinforces a positive mindset.
3. Open Dialogue: If appropriate, engage in an open dialogue with the person to gain a better understanding of their perspective and motivations.
4. Feedback and Learning: Consider providing constructive feedback when appropriate. Use frustrating situations as opportunities for personal growth and learning.

This tool offers a practical and empathetic approach to dealing with frustration in interpersonal relationships. By actively seeking positive qualities, understanding motivations, and finding common ground, individuals can transform frustration into opportunities for compassion, communication, and relationship building.

12) Never Be Overheard Complaining…Even to Yourself:

Anecdote: Imagine complaining as a leaky faucet. Drip by drip, negativity erodes your mindset.

Interpretation: Complaining amplifies negativity. Stoicism urges acceptance and constructive action. Complaining adds no value; it only amplifies problems.

Practical Tool: Establish a complaint-free day each week. Redirect complaints into solutions or gratitude. Redirect complaints into constructive actions or solutions.

The practical tool involves designating a complaint-free day each week and redirecting complaints into constructive actions or expressions of gratitude. The goal is to foster a positive mindset by transforming complaints into opportunities for solutions or appreciation.

Establish a Complaint-Free Day:

1. Choose a Specific Day: Select a specific day each week as your designated complaint-free day. This creates a focused time frame for practicing the tool.
2. Set Clear Intentions: Clearly define your intentions for the complaint-free day. Decide to refrain from expressing complaints or engaging in negative discussions.

Redirect Complaints into Solutions or Gratitude:

1. Pause and Reflect: When you feel the urge to complain, pause and reflect on the nature of the complaint. Consider whether it can be reframed into a constructive action or if there's an opportunity for gratitude.

2. Transform Complaints into Solutions: Instead of expressing complaints, channel that energy into identifying potential solutions or actionable steps to address the issue. Focus on problem-solving.

3. Express Gratitude: If the complaint is about a situation or person, redirect your thoughts towards expressions of gratitude. Find positive aspects or actions to appreciate.

How to Implement the Tool:

1. Start Small: Begin by implementing a complaint-free day on a smaller scale, and gradually extend it to a full day. This allows for a more manageable adjustment.

2. Create Reminders: Set reminders or visual cues to help you stay mindful of your commitment to a complaint-free day. This could be a note, an alarm, or any method that works for you.

3. Accountability Partner: Consider having an accountability partner who also participates in complaint-free days. Share your experiences and support each other in maintaining a positive mindset.

4. Reflect at the End of the Day: At the end of the complaint-free day, reflect on your experiences. Take note of any challenges, moments of success, and the overall impact on your mood and mindset.

Benefits of a Complaint-Free Day:

1. Positive Mindset Cultivation: Practicing a complaint-free day fosters the cultivation of a positive mindset, contributing to overall well-being.

2. Improved Problem-Solving Skills: Redirecting complaints into solutions enhances your problem-solving skills by encouraging proactive thinking.

3. Enhanced Gratitude: Transforming complaints into expressions of gratitude reinforces a sense of appreciation for positive aspects in your life.
4. Reduced Negativity: By refraining from complaints, you reduce negativity in your interactions and contribute to a more positive social environment.
5. Increased Awareness: The tool heightens your awareness of your own tendencies to complain, allowing you to make conscious choices about how you express dissatisfaction.

Adapt to Your Preferences:

1. Extend to Longer Periods: As you become more comfortable with complaint-free days, consider extending the practice to longer periods, such as complaint-free weeks or months.
2. Journaling: Keep a journal to document your experiences during complaint-free days. Record any insights, challenges, or positive outcomes.
3. Celebrate Successes: Celebrate your successes in maintaining a complaint-free mindset. Acknowledge the positive impact on your well-being and relationships.
4. Encourage Others: Encourage friends, family, or colleagues to join you in practicing complaint-free days. Collective efforts can create a more positive and supportive environment.

This tool offers a practical and actionable approach to fostering a positive mindset and constructive communication. By designating complaint-free days and redirecting complaints into solutions or expressions of gratitude, individuals can contribute to a more positive and uplifting personal and social atmosphere.

13) Two Ears, One Mouth…For a Reason (Zeno):

Anecdote: Think of a teacher and a student. Listening is a powerful tool for learning.

Interpretation: Listening cultivates understanding. Engage in active listening for richer connections. Listen more than you speak to gain wisdom.

Practical Tool: Practice the 2:1 ratio. Listen twice as much as you speak in conversations. Practice active listening, absorbing information before responding.

The practical tool involves practicing a 2:1 ratio in conversations, emphasizing listening twice as much as you speak. This tool encourages active listening, where the focus is on absorbing information from others before responding.

Practice the 2:1 Ratio:

1. Listen Twice as Much: The core principle of this tool is to consciously aim for a 2:1 ratio, meaning that you spend twice as much time listening as you do speaking in conversations.
2. Active Listening: Active listening goes beyond simply hearing words. It involves fully engaging with the speaker, focusing on their words, tone, and non-verbal cues to gain a deeper understanding.

How to Implement the Tool:

1. Conscious Awareness: Develop a conscious awareness of your speaking-to-listening ratio. Pay attention to your contributions in conversations and make a deliberate effort to listen more.

2. Avoid Interrupting: Resist the urge to interrupt while others are speaking. Allow them to express themselves fully before responding.
3. Ask Open-Ended Questions: Encourage others to share more by asking open-ended questions. This promotes a more extended and in-depth exchange of ideas.
4. Maintain Eye Contact: Maintain eye contact with the speaker to convey attentiveness and interest. Non-verbal cues are crucial in demonstrating active listening.
5. Reflective Listening: Practice reflective listening by paraphrasing or summarizing what the speaker has said. This not only shows understanding but also allows for clarification.

Benefits of the 2:1 Ratio:

1. Improved Understanding: By listening more than speaking, you gain a better understanding of the perspectives, opinions, and information shared by others.
2. Enhanced Relationships: Actively listening fosters stronger relationships by demonstrating respect and genuine interest in others' thoughts and experiences.
3. Conflict Prevention: Engaging in active listening helps prevent misunderstandings and conflicts by ensuring that you fully comprehend others' viewpoints before responding.
4. Increased Empathy: The 2:1 ratio promotes empathy as you invest time in truly understanding the emotions and perspectives of those you are communicating with.

5. Effective Communication: This tool contributes to more effective communication, as it encourages a thoughtful and measured approach to conversations.

Adapt to Your Preferences:

1. Set Listening Goals: Set specific listening goals for yourself, such as increasing the duration of focused listening during each conversation.
2. Feedback and Self-Reflection: Seek feedback from others on your listening skills and reflect on your own performance. Continuous improvement is key.
3. Practice Mindful Listening: Incorporate mindfulness practices to stay present and fully engaged in conversations. Minimize distractions and give your full attention to the speaker.
4. Variations in Different Contexts: Acknowledge that the 2:1 ratio may vary in different contexts. Adjust your approach based on the nature of the conversation and the individuals involved.
5. Encourage Others to Share: Actively encourage others to share their thoughts and opinions. Create an environment that values diverse perspectives.

This tool provides a practical and actionable approach to enhance communication skills by prioritizing active listening. By consciously practicing the 2:1 ratio, individuals can foster better understanding, build stronger relationships, and contribute to more effective and empathetic communication.

14) There Is Always Something You Can Do:

Anecdote: Picture a maze. Even if paths seem blocked, there's always a way forward.

Interpretation: Despite adversity, agency lies in choosing our response, fostering resilience. Focus on solutions rather than obstacles.

Practical Tool: When facing challenges, identify one action within your control, no matter how small. When faced with challenges, identify actionable steps rather than dwelling on limitations.

The practical tool involves a two-step process when facing challenges: identifying one action within your control and focusing on actionable steps rather than dwelling on limitations. This tool encourages a proactive and solution-oriented mindset.

Two-Step Approach to Facing Challenges:

1. Identify One Action within Your Control: When confronted with challenges, the first step is to identify at least one action or step that is within your control. This could be a small, manageable task that contributes to addressing the challenge.

2. Focus on Actionable Steps, Not Limitations: The second step involves shifting your focus away from dwelling on limitations or the magnitude of the challenge. Instead, concentrate on actionable steps and solutions that you can implement.

How to Implement the Tool:

1. Assess the Challenge: Take a moment to assess the challenge you are facing. Understand the nature of the problem and any constraints involved.

2. Identify Actions within Your Control: Break down the challenge and identify at least one action or step that you have control over. This could be a specific task or decision that contributes to addressing the challenge.

3. Prioritize Actionable Steps: Prioritize actionable steps over dwelling on limitations. List down practical and achievable tasks that can move you forward in addressing the challenge.

4. Create a Plan: Develop a plan outlining the actionable steps you've identified. Consider the sequence and dependencies of these steps to create a roadmap for addressing the challenge.

5. Take Immediate Action: Implement the identified actions as soon as possible. Taking immediate action helps build momentum and demonstrates a proactive approach.

Benefits of Focusing on Actionable Steps:

1. Proactive Problem-Solving: The tool promotes a proactive mindset by encouraging individuals to focus on practical steps and solutions.

2. Reduced Overwhelm: Breaking down challenges into actionable steps reduces the feeling of overwhelm associated with facing a complex problem.

3. Increased Confidence: Taking control of actionable steps boosts confidence, as individuals see tangible progress in addressing the challenge.

4. Enhanced Productivity: By concentrating on actionable steps, individuals can enhance productivity and make steady progress towards resolving the challenge.

5. Adaptability: The tool encourages adaptability by shifting the focus from limitations to actionable steps, fostering a more flexible and solution-oriented mindset.

Adapt to Your Preferences:

1. Involve Others: Seek input and collaboration from others when identifying actionable steps. Collective brainstorming can yield a broader range of ideas.
2. Celebrate Small Wins: Acknowledge and celebrate each small win as you complete actionable steps. This positive reinforcement reinforces a proactive approach.
3. Reassess and Adjust: Periodically reassess the challenge and your progress. If needed, adjust your plan and identify new actionable steps based on evolving circumstances.
4. Seek Support: If the challenge is particularly complex, seek support or guidance from mentors, colleagues, or friends. External perspectives can offer valuable insights.
5. Incorporate Reflection: Include reflection in your process. After implementing actionable steps, reflect on what worked well and what could be improved for future challenges.

This tool serves as a practical guide for navigating challenges with a proactive and solution-focused mindset. By identifying one action within your control and concentrating on actionable steps, individuals can approach challenges with confidence, reduce feelings of overwhelm, and steadily make progress towards resolution.

15) Don't Compare Yourself to Others:

Anecdote: Consider a garden. Each flower blooms in its own time and way.

Interpretation: Focus on self-improvement rather than comparison, fostering gratitude for your unique journey. Your journey is unique; avoid the trap of comparison.

Practical Tool: Create personal benchmarks. Compare present self to past self, not others. Celebrate your progress and focus on personal growth, not external benchmarks.

The practical tool involves creating personal benchmarks for self-evaluation, comparing your present self to your past self rather than others. The focus is on celebrating personal progress and fostering a mindset centered on individual growth rather than external benchmarks.

Create Personal Benchmarks:

1. Set Individual Goals: Establish personal goals that are meaningful and relevant to your aspirations, values, and areas of improvement. These goals become your benchmarks for self-evaluation.
2. Define Success on Your Terms: Define what success means to you based on your personal values and objectives. This ensures that your benchmarks align with your unique definition of achievement.

Compare Present Self to Past Self:

1. Reflect on Personal Growth: Regularly reflect on your journey and the progress you've made over time. Identify areas where

you have grown, developed skills, or achieved personal milestones.

2. Avoid External Comparisons: Resist the temptation to compare yourself to others. Instead, focus on your personal evolution and how far you've come from your past self.

Celebrate Progress and Personal Growth:

1. Acknowledge Achievements: Celebrate your achievements, both big and small. Acknowledge the effort you've invested in reaching your goals and recognize the progress you've made.

2. Shift Focus from External Benchmarks: Redirect your attention away from external benchmarks or societal expectations. Embrace a mindset that values your personal growth journey over external validations.

How to Implement the Tool:

1. Define Personal Goals: Clearly define personal goals that align with your values and aspirations. These could be related to career, personal development, relationships, or any other aspect of your life.

2. Establish Benchmarks: Break down your goals into specific benchmarks or milestones. These serve as indicators of progress and success along your personal growth journey.

3. Regular Self-Reflection: Schedule regular moments for self-reflection. Assess your current status in relation to your past self and evaluate the progress you've made toward your benchmarks.

4. Celebrate Achievements: Actively celebrate your achievements. Whether it's reaching a milestone, overcoming a challenge, or

developing a new skill, take time to acknowledge your accomplishments.

5. Embrace Continuous Learning: Cultivate a mindset of continuous learning and improvement. Use setbacks as opportunities to learn and adjust your approach, fostering resilience and adaptability.

Benefits of Personal Benchmarks and Self-Reflection:

1. Individualized Growth: Personal benchmarks ensure that your growth journey is tailored to your individual needs and aspirations.

2. Increased Motivation: Regular self-reflection and celebration of achievements contribute to increased motivation to pursue personal goals.

3. Enhanced Self-Awareness: The process of self-reflection fosters self-awareness, allowing you to better understand your strengths, weaknesses, and areas for improvement.

4. Resilience Building: Acknowledging and learning from setbacks builds resilience, as you develop the ability to overcome challenges and adapt to changing circumstances.

5. Reduced External Pressures: By focusing on personal benchmarks, you reduce the impact of external pressures and societal expectations, fostering a more authentic and fulfilling growth journey.

Adapt to Your Preferences:

1. Incorporate Journaling: Keep a journal to document your personal growth journey. Record achievements, challenges, and reflections to track your progress.

2. Seek Feedback from Within: Regularly check in with yourself to assess your satisfaction and fulfillment in various areas of your life. Use this internal feedback to guide your personal growth goals.
3. Share Your Journey: Share your personal growth journey with trusted friends, mentors, or family members. Their perspectives and support can provide valuable insights and encouragement.
4. Adjust Goals as Needed: Be open to adjusting your personal goals and benchmarks based on evolving priorities and aspirations. Adaptability is key to a dynamic growth journey.
5. Connect with a Community: Join a community or network of individuals with similar personal growth aspirations. Sharing experiences and insights can enhance your own journey and provide mutual support.

This tool emphasizes the importance of creating individualized benchmarks for personal growth, focusing on self-reflection, and celebrating progress. By comparing your present self to your past self and embracing a mindset centered on personal development, you cultivate a fulfilling and authentic journey towards your goals.

16) Live as if You've Died and Come Back (Every Minute Is Bonus Time):

Anecdote: Imagine a second chance at life. Embrace each moment as a gift.

Interpretation: Live with gratitude, appreciating each moment as a bonus, not to be taken for granted. Live fully, appreciating the preciousness of time.

Practical Tool: Engage in activities as if they are your last, savoring the present moment. Approach life with gratitude, mindful of the opportunities each moment presents.

The practical tool involves engaging in activities as if they are your last, savoring the present moment, and approaching life with gratitude. The focus is on cultivating mindfulness, being fully present, and appreciating the opportunities each moment offers.

Engage in Activities as if They Are Your Last:

1. Mindful Presence: Approach each activity with a heightened sense of awareness and mindfulness. Be fully present in the moment, immersing yourself in the experience.
2. Savor the Present Moment: Practice savoring the present moment by paying attention to your senses, emotions, and surroundings. Engage your senses fully to appreciate the richness of the experience.

Approach Life with Gratitude:

1. Cultivate a Grateful Mindset: Foster a mindset of gratitude by acknowledging and appreciating the opportunities and blessings present in your life. Focus on what you have rather than what you lack.
2. Express Gratitude Daily: Take time each day to express gratitude. This could involve keeping a gratitude journal, where you write down things you're thankful for, or verbally expressing gratitude to others.

How to Implement the Tool:

1. Mindful Engagement: Before starting an activity, take a moment to center yourself. Be aware of your surroundings, your

emotions, and the purpose of the activity. Engage with intention and focus.

2. Use Your Senses: Actively use your senses to experience the present moment. Notice the colors, sounds, textures, and smells around you. Engage your senses to create a vivid and memorable experience.

3. Appreciate Simple Moments: Practice appreciating even the simplest moments in life. Whether it's a quiet morning, a shared meal, or a walk in nature, find joy and meaning in these everyday experiences.

4. Express Gratitude Silently: In the midst of an activity, silently express gratitude for the opportunity to engage in that moment. Acknowledge the positive aspects and the uniqueness of the experience.

5. Reflect on Daily Blessings: At the end of each day, reflect on the blessings and positive moments you've experienced. This reflective practice reinforces a mindset of gratitude.

Benefits of Mindful Engagement and Gratitude:

1. Increased Joy and Fulfillment: Engaging in activities mindfully and expressing gratitude contribute to increased joy and fulfillment in daily life.

2. Reduced Stress and Anxiety: Mindfulness and gratitude practices have been shown to reduce stress and anxiety by promoting a focus on the present moment and positive aspects of life.

3. Enhanced Relationships: Being fully present in interactions and expressing gratitude can strengthen relationships by fostering a deeper connection and appreciation for others.

4. Improved Mental Well-being: Incorporating mindfulness and gratitude into daily life contributes to improved mental well-being, promoting a positive outlook and resilience.

5. Cultivation of Positive Habits: Regular engagement in mindful and grateful practices helps cultivate positive habits that contribute to a more optimistic and fulfilling lifestyle.

Adapt to Your Preferences:

1. Create Mindful Rituals: Establish mindful rituals that align with your interests and daily routine. These rituals can serve as reminders to engage in activities with presence and gratitude.

2. Share Moments with Others: Invite others to share in moments of mindfulness and gratitude. Engaging in these practices together can strengthen social bonds and create shared positive experiences.

3. Explore Mindful Activities: Explore activities that naturally lend themselves to mindfulness, such as meditation, yoga, or mindful walks. Find what resonates with you and incorporate it into your routine.

4. Personalize Gratitude Practices: Personalize your gratitude practices to suit your preferences. Whether it's through writing, verbal expressions, or visualizations, find the approach that feels most authentic to you.

5. Integrate Mindfulness into Challenges: When faced with challenges, approach them mindfully and with gratitude for the opportunities they present for growth and learning.

This tool encourages individuals to approach life with a sense of mindfulness and gratitude, savoring each moment and appreciating the blessings in daily experiences. By incorporating these practices into daily life, individuals can enhance their overall well-being and cultivate a positive and fulfilling mindset.

17) "The Best Revenge Is Not to Be Like That." Marcus Aurelius:

Anecdote: Picture a conflict. Rising above negativity is the ultimate victory.

Interpretation: Responding with virtue is the ultimate victory, transcending petty retaliations. Respond to adversity with virtue, not retaliation.

Practical Tool: In moments of betrayal, pause and choose a response aligned with your values. When faced with hostility, choose a response that aligns with your values.

The practical tool involves a two-step process when encountering moments of betrayal or hostility: pausing to reflect and choosing a response aligned with your values. This tool encourages individuals to approach challenging situations with mindfulness and make intentional decisions that align with their personal values.

Two-Step Approach to Challenging Situations:

1. Pause and Reflect: In moments of betrayal or hostility, the first step is to pause before reacting. Take a moment to collect your thoughts, regulate your emotions, and create space for reflection.
2. Choose a Values-Aligned Response: After the pause, deliberately choose a response that aligns with your values. Consider how your actions and words can reflect your principles and contribute to a constructive resolution.

How to Implement the Tool:

1. Recognize the Emotions: Acknowledge and recognize the emotions that arise in response to betrayal or hostility. Be aware of your initial reactions and the potential impact they may have.

2. Take a Breath: Physically pause by taking a deep breath. This simple act helps in calming the nervous system and creating a moment of stillness before responding.

3. Reflect on Values: Reflect on your core values. Consider what principles and beliefs are important to you in this situation. Your values serve as a compass for guiding your response.

4. Consider Long-Term Goals: Think about your long-term goals and the kind of person you want to be. Consider how your response in this moment can contribute to your personal growth and well-being.

5. Choose a Thoughtful Response: Based on your reflection, choose a response that is thoughtful, measured, and in alignment with your values. This might involve expressing your feelings, setting boundaries, or seeking resolution through dialogue.

Benefits of Values-Aligned Responses:

1. Maintained Integrity: Choosing responses aligned with your values helps maintain your personal integrity, ensuring that your actions are consistent with your principles.

2. Effective Conflict Resolution: Values-aligned responses contribute to more effective conflict resolution by fostering open communication and understanding.

3. Enhanced Emotional Regulation: Pausing and choosing a values-aligned response aids in emotional regulation, preventing impulsive reactions that may exacerbate the situation.
4. Personal Growth: Consciously responding in accordance with your values promotes personal growth, resilience, and a deeper understanding of yourself.
5. Positive Impact on Relationships: Values-aligned responses contribute to building and maintaining positive relationships, as they reflect respect and consideration for others.

Adapt to Your Preferences:

1. Develop a Values Framework: Establish a clear understanding of your core values. This framework serves as a guide for decision-making in challenging situations.
2. Practice Mindfulness Techniques: Incorporate mindfulness techniques, such as meditation or deep breathing, into your routine. These practices can enhance your ability to pause and reflect in the heat of the moment.
3. Seek Support and Perspective: If needed, seek support from friends, family, or mentors. Discussing the situation with others can provide additional perspectives and insights.
4. Establish Healthy Boundaries: Prioritize the establishment of healthy boundaries. Clearly communicate your boundaries to others, and be assertive in maintaining them in moments of betrayal or hostility.
5. Continuous Learning: Approach challenging situations as opportunities for continuous learning. Reflect on each experience

and consider how it contributes to your personal and interpersonal growth.

This tool empowers individuals to respond thoughtfully and intentionally in moments of betrayal or hostility, ensuring that their actions align with their values. By incorporating this approach into daily life, individuals can navigate challenging situations with greater resilience, integrity, and a focus on long-term well-being.

18) Be Strict with Yourself and Tolerant with Others:

Anecdote: Think of a coach. Push yourself to excel, but understand others have different journeys.

Interpretation: Balance self-improvement with compassion, recognizing everyone is on their own journey. Hold high standards for yourself while practicing empathy for others.

Practical Tool: Set high standards for yourself but practice patience and empathy toward others. Set personal expectations, but be compassionate when others fall short.

The practical tool involves setting high standards for oneself while practicing patience and empathy towards others. This tool encourages individuals to maintain personal expectations and standards, yet approach interactions with others with understanding and compassion.

Two-Part Approach to Standards and Empathy:

1. Set High Standards for Yourself: Establish clear and ambitious standards for your own performance, behavior, and goals. Strive for excellence and continuous improvement in various aspects of your life.

2. Practice Patience and Empathy Toward Others: Extend patience and empathy when dealing with others, recognizing that everyone has their own strengths, challenges, and circumstances. Understand that people may fall short of expectations at times.

How to Implement the Tool:

1. Define Personal Standards: Clearly define your personal standards and expectations. Identify areas where you want to excel and set goals that challenge you to continually improve.
2. Hold Yourself Accountable: Hold yourself accountable to the high standards you've set. Be disciplined in your efforts to meet and exceed your own expectations.
3. Cultivate Patience: Practice patience in your interactions with others. Understand that people have different abilities, timelines, and priorities. Allow room for growth and development.
4. Empathize with Others: Cultivate empathy by putting yourself in others' shoes. Consider their perspectives, challenges, and circumstances. This helps in understanding why they might not meet certain standards at a given moment.
5. Provide Constructive Feedback: When working with others, offer constructive feedback rather than criticism. Focus on areas for improvement and provide support to help them meet expectations.

Benefits of Balancing Standards and Empathy:

1. Personal Growth: Setting high standards for yourself fosters personal growth and development as you continually strive for excellence.

2. Effective Leadership: Balancing standards with empathy is crucial for effective leadership. Leaders who understand and support their team members create a positive and productive work environment.
3. Positive Relationships: Practicing patience and empathy in relationships builds trust and fosters positive connections. People are more likely to collaborate and communicate openly in such environments.
4. Cultivation of Resilience: Balancing high standards with empathy contributes to the cultivation of resilience. This approach helps individuals bounce back from setbacks and challenges.
5. Harmonious Team Dynamics: In team settings, a balance of personal standards and empathy contributes to harmonious dynamics. Individuals feel motivated to perform well while knowing that support is available when needed.

Adapt to Your Preferences:

1. Regular Self-Reflection: Incorporate regular self-reflection into your routine. Assess your progress, evaluate whether your standards are realistic, and consider how you can enhance your empathy towards others.
2. Communicate Expectations Clearly: When working with others, communicate expectations clearly. Ensure that everyone understands the standards to be met and the support available.
3. Encourage Open Communication: Foster open communication within your personal and professional relationships. Encourage others to share their challenges and seek assistance when needed.

4. Offer Support and Resources: If others are struggling to meet expectations, offer support and resources to help them succeed. Collaborate on finding solutions rather than placing blame.

5. Adapt Standards as Needed: Be flexible in adapting your personal standards based on evolving circumstances. Recognize when adjustments are necessary and approach changes with a growth mindset.

By implementing this practical tool, individuals can maintain high personal standards while fostering a compassionate and understanding approach towards others. This balance contributes to personal growth, positive relationships, and effective collaboration in various aspects of life.

19) Put Every Impression, Emotion, to the Test Before Acting on It:

Anecdote: Imagine emotions as messengers. Evaluate their validity before acting.

Interpretation: Emotions can cloud judgment. Evaluate them and assess their relevance. before allowing them to influence actions.

Practical Tool: Implement a "10-second rule." Pause for reflection before acting on intense emotions. Pause and analyze your emotions, ensuring your actions align with reason.

The practical tool involves implementing a "10-second rule" in moments of intense emotions. This tool encourages individuals to pause for reflection before acting, taking a brief moment to analyze their emotions and ensuring that their actions align with reason. Implementing the 10-Second Rule:

1. Recognize Intense Emotions: When faced with intense emotions such as anger, frustration, or anxiety, recognize the emotional state you are in. Be aware of the intensity of your feelings.
2. Initiate the 10-Second Pause: As soon as you become aware of intense emotions, initiate the 10-second rule. This involves taking a brief pause before responding or taking any action.
3. Breathe and Center Yourself: Use the pause to take a few deep breaths and center yourself. This helps in calming the nervous system and creating a mental space for reflection.
4. Analyze Your Emotions: During the 10-second pause, analyze your emotions. Consider the source of your feelings, the triggers, and the potential impact of your actions.
5. Ensure Alignment with Reason: Assess whether your initial impulse aligns with reason and logic. Evaluate whether your actions, if taken immediately, would contribute positively to the situation or escalate tensions.

How to Implement the Tool:
1. Build Awareness of Triggers: Develop self-awareness by identifying common triggers that lead to intense emotions. Recognize patterns and situations that tend to provoke strong reactions.
2. Practice Mindfulness: Incorporate mindfulness practices into your routine to enhance your ability to stay present and self-aware. Mindfulness can contribute to a more measured response in intense emotional moments.

3. Set a Mental Timer: Mentally set a timer for 10 seconds when you sense intense emotions rising. Use this time to collect your thoughts and prepare for a more deliberate response.

4. Consider Consequences: Reflect on the potential consequences of your immediate actions. Consider how your response might impact relationships, your well-being, and the overall situation.

5. Seek Perspective: If possible, seek perspective from others or consider alternative viewpoints. This can provide valuable insights and help you make a more informed decision.

Benefits of the 10-Second Rule:

1. Emotional Regulation: The 10-second rule contributes to emotional regulation by providing a brief period for the intensity of emotions to subside, allowing for a more composed response.

2. Reduced Impulsivity: By implementing this tool, individuals reduce impulsive reactions that may be driven by intense emotions. This leads to more thoughtful and intentional actions.

3. Improved Decision-Making: Taking a moment to analyze emotions and ensure alignment with reason enhances decision-making in challenging situations, leading to more effective outcomes.

4. Enhanced Communication: The 10-second rule fosters better communication by allowing individuals to respond in a manner that is thoughtful and considerate, rather than reactive.

5. Conflict Prevention: The tool serves as a preventive measure for conflicts by giving individuals the opportunity to choose responses that de-escalate situations rather than exacerbate them.

Adapt to Your Preferences:

1. Adjust the Timeframe: Depending on the intensity of emotions and the situation, consider adjusting the timeframe of the rule. It could be a 5-second or 15-second rule based on what works best for you.
2. Incorporate Reflection Practices: Develop a habit of reflecting on your emotions regularly, not just in intense moments. This practice enhances self-awareness and contributes to overall emotional well-being.
3. Combine with Other Techniques: Combine the 10-second rule with other emotional regulation techniques, such as positive affirmations or visualization exercises. This creates a holistic approach to managing emotions.
4. Share the Rule with Others: If appropriate, share the 10-second rule with those around you. Encouraging a collective commitment to thoughtful responses can positively impact group dynamics.
5. Create a Physical Cue: Associate a physical cue, such as touching your fingers together or taking a specific posture, with the 10-second rule. This can serve as a reminder to pause and reflect in emotionally charged moments.

By incorporating the 10-second rule into daily life, individuals can navigate intense emotional moments with greater composure and reason. This tool empowers individuals to respond thoughtfully, fostering better relationships and effective decision-making in various aspects of life.

20) Learn Something from Everyone:

Anecdote: Picture a diverse library. Each person holds a unique book of wisdom.

Interpretation: Embrace a humble mindset, recognizing opportunities for learning from every person. Every interaction is an opportunity for learning.

Practical Tool: Engage in conversations with diverse individuals, seeking to understand their perspectives. Approach conversations with curiosity, seeking to gain insights from others.

The practical tool encourages engaging in conversations with diverse individuals, approaching these interactions with curiosity and a genuine desire to understand their perspectives. The focus is on fostering an open-minded and inclusive approach to communication.

Engaging in Conversations with Diverse Individuals:

1. Diverse Interactions: Actively seek out conversations with individuals from diverse backgrounds, perspectives, and experiences. This diversity can include differences in culture, beliefs, age, gender, and more.

2. Create Inclusive Spaces: Foster environments that are inclusive and welcoming to a variety of perspectives. Encourage open dialogue where individuals feel comfortable sharing their thoughts and experiences.

Approaching Conversations with Curiosity:

1. Curiosity as a Mindset: Cultivate curiosity as a mindset when entering conversations. Approach interactions with a genuine

interest in learning and understanding the unique perspectives of others.

2. Ask Open-Ended Questions: Pose open-ended questions that invite individuals to share more about their experiences and viewpoints. This encourages deeper and more meaningful conversations.

How to Implement the Tool:

1. Expand Your Social Circles: Actively seek to expand your social circles by engaging with individuals from different backgrounds. Attend events, join groups, or participate in activities that attract diverse participants.

2. Listen Actively: Practice active listening during conversations. Give your full attention to the speaker, avoid interrupting, and show genuine interest in what they are expressing.

3. Express Empathy: Demonstrate empathy by trying to understand the emotions and perspectives of others. Put yourself in their shoes and validate their experiences.

4. Suspend Judgment: Suspend judgment and preconceived notions when engaging in conversations. Allow individuals to express themselves freely without imposing your own biases.

5. Share Your Own Perspectives: While seeking to understand others, also share your own perspectives and experiences. This creates a reciprocal exchange of insights and promotes mutual understanding.

Benefits of Conversing with Diverse Individuals:

1. Broadened Perspectives: Engaging with diverse individuals, broadens your own perspectives, exposing you to different ways of thinking, living, and understanding the world.
2. Cultural Competence: Conversations with individuals from diverse backgrounds contribute to cultural competence, enhancing your ability to navigate and appreciate cultural differences.
3. Increased Empathy: Actively seeking to understand diverse perspectives fosters empathy. You develop a deeper appreciation for the varied experiences and challenges faced by others.
4. Enhanced Communication Skills: Regular engagement in diverse conversations hones your communication skills. You become adept at expressing your ideas clearly while also actively listening to others.
5. Conflict Resolution Skills: Understanding diverse perspectives equips you with valuable conflict resolution skills. You learn to navigate disagreements with respect and openness.

Adapt to Your Preferences:

1. Participate in Cross-Cultural Events: Attend events that celebrate diversity and bring together people from various cultural backgrounds. These environments provide rich opportunities for diverse conversations.
2. Join Discussion Groups: Join discussion groups or forums that focus on topics of interest where diverse perspectives are valued. Online platforms and local community groups can be excellent spaces for such interactions.

3. Read Widely: Expand your knowledge and understanding by reading books, articles, and publications from diverse authors. This can inform your conversations and deepen your appreciation for different viewpoints.
4. Attend Workshops on Inclusion: Attend workshops or training sessions on diversity and inclusion. These experiences can provide valuable insights and tools for navigating conversations in diverse settings.
5. Reflect on Your Biases: Regularly reflect on your own biases and assumptions. Acknowledging and addressing your biases allows you to approach conversations with a more open and unbiased mindset.

By incorporating this tool into your daily interactions, you contribute to creating a more inclusive and understanding world. Engaging in conversations with diverse individuals with curiosity and an open heart fosters connections, broadens perspectives, and promotes a culture of respect and appreciation for differences.

21) Focus on Process, Not Outcomes:

Anecdote: Envision a sculptor at work. Mastery comes from the dedication to the process, not just the end result.

Interpretation: Outcomes are beyond our control. Mastery lies in dedicating ourselves to the process. Concentrate on the journey, not just the destination.

Practical Tool: Set process-oriented goals, emphasizing the journey over the destination. Set goals but derive satisfaction from the effort put in, not just the final achievement.

The practical tool involves setting process-oriented goals, prioritizing the journey over the destination. This approach encourages individuals to focus on the effort, learning, and experiences along the way, deriving satisfaction not only from achieving the final goal but also from the progress made during the journey.

Setting Process-Oriented Goals:

1. Define Goals with a Focus on Process: When setting goals, place emphasis on the processes and actions involved rather than solely on the end result. Consider the steps, strategies, and habits that contribute to progress.

2. Identify Key Milestones: Break down larger goals into smaller, manageable milestones. These milestones serve as indicators of progress and allow for a more tangible sense of achievement throughout the journey.

Emphasizing the Journey Over the Destination:

1. Shift Mindset Toward Enjoying the Process: Cultivate a mindset that values and enjoys the process of working towards a goal. Appreciate the learning, growth, and experiences that come with each step of the journey.

2. Derive Satisfaction from Effort and Progress: Find satisfaction in the effort you put into pursuing your goals and the progress you make along the way. Celebrate small victories and recognize the value of the journey itself.

How to Implement the Tool:

1. Define Clear Process-Oriented Steps: Clearly outline the steps and actions required to achieve your goal. Focus on what needs

to be done in the present moment rather than fixating solely on the end outcome.

2. Create a Progress Journal: Keep a journal to document your progress, experiences, and insights throughout the journey. This allows you to reflect on the value of the process and the lessons learned.

3. Celebrate Small Wins: Acknowledge and celebrate small victories and achievements along the way. Recognize the effort, dedication, and resilience that contribute to your progress.

4. Learn from Challenges: View challenges and setbacks as opportunities for learning and growth. Embrace the lessons they offer and adapt your approach, recognizing that the journey includes both successes and obstacles.

5. Incorporate Continuous Improvement: Continuously assess and refine your processes as you move forward. Seek ways to improve and optimize your strategies, fostering a commitment to ongoing learning and development.

Benefits of Emphasizing the Journey:

1. Sustained Motivation: Focusing on the journey sustains motivation by providing ongoing sources of satisfaction and fulfillment throughout the process.

2. Increased Resilience: Embracing challenges and setbacks as part of the journey builds resilience. Individuals become more adaptable and better equipped to navigate obstacles.

3. Enhanced Enjoyment of the Process: Valuing the journey over the destination enhances the overall enjoyment of the process.

Individuals find fulfillment in the day-to-day experiences and efforts invested.

4. Long-Term Consistency: Process-oriented goals contribute to long-term consistency. Individuals are more likely to sustain their efforts over time when they find value and satisfaction in the journey.

5. Holistic Development: The focus on the journey promotes holistic development. Individuals grow not only in terms of achieving specific goals but also in their skills, mindset, and overall personal development.

Adapt to Your Preferences:

1. Set Short-Term Process Goals: Establish short-term process goals that align with your larger objectives. These smaller goals provide more frequent opportunities for celebrating progress.

2. Engage in Reflective Practices: Incorporate reflective practices, such as mindfulness or journaling, into your routine. Regular reflection enhances your awareness of the journey and fosters a deeper connection to the present moment.

3. Collaborate with Others: Share your journey and collaborate with others who have similar goals. Collective efforts and support contribute to a more enriching and enjoyable experience.

4. Experiment with New Approaches: Be open to experimenting with different approaches and strategies. Embrace a mindset of curiosity and continuous improvement, exploring what works best for you.

5. Set Meaningful Intentions: Alongside specific goals, set meaningful intentions for your journey. Consider the values and principles that guide your actions, adding depth and purpose to the process.

By implementing this practical tool, individuals shift their focus from a fixation on end results to a more appreciative and fulfilling experience of the journey itself. Emphasizing the process over the destination fosters sustained motivation, resilience, and a holistic approach to personal and professional growth.

22) Define What Success Means to You:

Anecdote: Picture a diverse art gallery. Success takes many forms; find what resonates with you.

Interpretation: Personalize success. Align goals with your values, avoiding external validation. Create your definition of success rather than adopting societal standards.

Practical Tool: Create a vision board that reflects your unique definition of success. List personal values and goals, forming the basis of your unique definition of success.

The practical tool involves creating a vision board to visually represent your unique definition of success. This tool combines the visualization of goals and values, providing a tangible and inspiring representation of what success means to you.

Creating a Vision Board for Success:

1. Define Personal Values: Begin by identifying and defining your personal values. These are the principles and beliefs that guide your decisions and actions. Consider values related to various aspects of life, such as relationships, career, personal growth, and well-being.

2. Set Personal Goals: Outline specific and meaningful goals that align with your values. These goals should reflect what success

looks like for you in different areas of your life. Ensure that they are realistic, measurable, and time-bound.

3. Select Visual Representations: Choose images, words, and symbols that visually represent your values and goals. These can be pictures from magazines, printed quotes, drawings, or any visual elements that resonate with your unique vision of success.

4. Create the Vision Board: Arrange the selected visuals on a board or any surface in a way that is visually appealing to you. You can organize them based on different categories, themes, or a chronological progression.

5. Incorporate Affirmations: Include affirmations or positive statements that reinforce your beliefs and aspirations. These affirmations serve as powerful reminders of the mindset you want to cultivate on your journey to success.

How to Implement the Tool:

1. Regularly Update Your Vision Board: Review and update your vision board periodically. As your values and goals evolve, adjust the visuals to reflect your current aspirations and priorities.

2. Place the Vision Board in a Visible Location: Keep your vision board in a visible location where you can see it daily. This could be in your workspace, bedroom, or any area you frequent. Regular exposure reinforces your commitment to your unique definition of success.

3. Reflect on Each Element: Take time to reflect on each element of your vision board. Consider why each image or word is significant to you and how it contributes to your overall vision of success.

4. Visualize Success: Use the vision board as a tool for visualization. Close your eyes, visualize yourself achieving your goals, and immerse yourself in the emotions associated with success.

5. Share Your Vision: If comfortable, share your vision board with trusted friends, family, or mentors. Explaining your vision to others can provide valuable insights and support, fostering a sense of accountability.

Benefits of Creating a Vision Board:

1. Clarity of Purpose: Creating a vision board helps clarify your purpose and aspirations. It provides a tangible representation of what success means to you in different areas of your life.

2. Motivation and Inspiration: The visual nature of a vision board serves as a constant source of motivation and inspiration. It reminds you of your goals, values, and the vision you are working towards.

3. Alignment with Values: By including your personal values, the vision board ensures that your pursuit of success aligns with your core beliefs. This alignment contributes to a sense of authenticity and fulfillment.

4. Goal Visualization: Visualization is a powerful technique for goal achievement. The act of creating and regularly viewing your vision board enhances your ability to visualize success, making it feel more achievable.

5. Positive Mindset Reinforcement: Affirmations and positive statements on the vision board reinforce a positive mindset.

Regular exposure to these affirmations contributes to the cultivation of a success-oriented mindset.

Adapt to Your Preferences:

1. Digital Vision Boards: If you prefer a digital approach, create a vision board using online tools or apps. This allows for easy updates and sharing with others.

2. Include Short-Term and Long-Term Goals: Incorporate both short-term and long-term goals on your vision board. This provides a comprehensive view of your journey to success.

3. Collage or Artistic Expression: Express your vision through artistic means. Consider creating a collage, painting, or any other form of artistic expression that resonates with you.

4. Personalize Your Space: Personalize your physical environment beyond the vision board. Surround yourself with elements that align with your vision of success, creating an environment that fosters motivation and focus.

5. Use Multiple Boards for Different Areas: If you have diverse goals and values in different areas of your life, consider creating multiple vision boards. Each board can represent a specific category, allowing for a more detailed and focused visualization.

By creating a vision board that reflects your unique definition of success, you empower yourself to stay focused on your goals and values. The visual representation serves as a daily reminder of what you are working towards and inspires a positive and purposeful mindset.

23) Find a Way to Love Everything That Happens (Amor Fati):

Anecdote: Imagine a puzzle. Embrace challenges as pieces forming the beautiful mosaic of your life.

Interpretation: Acceptance of all experiences, good or bad, leads to inner tranquility and growth. Cultivate love for all experiences, even the difficult ones.

Practical Tool: In challenging situations, seek the lesson or opportunity for growth. Reframe challenges as opportunities for growth and learning.

The practical tool involves adopting a mindset that seeks lessons or opportunities for growth in challenging situations. This approach encourages individuals to reframe challenges, viewing them not as obstacles but as valuable experiences that contribute to personal and professional development.

Seeking Lessons in Challenging Situations:

1. Mindset Shift: Cultivate a mindset that views challenges as opportunities for learning and growth. Embrace the belief that every difficult situation carries valuable lessons and potential for personal development.

2. Reframe Challenges: When faced with a challenge, consciously reframe it in your mind. Instead of seeing it as a setback, view it as a chance to acquire new skills, insights, or perspectives.

How to Implement the Tool:

1. Reflect on Challenges: Take time to reflect on challenging situations. Consider the specific difficulties you are facing and

explore what lessons or opportunities for growth may be hidden within them.

2. Ask Yourself Questions: Pose questions that prompt reflection on the challenge. Ask yourself what you can learn from the situation, how it aligns with your goals, and what skills or qualities you can develop in response.

3. Identify Personal Growth Areas: Identify areas of personal growth that may be relevant to the challenge. This could include improving resilience, problem-solving skills, adaptability, communication, or other qualities that contribute to personal and professional success.

4. Set Learning Objectives: Transform challenges into intentional learning opportunities by setting learning objectives. Determine specific skills or knowledge you aim to gain through navigating the challenge.

5. Document Insights: Keep a journal or document insights gained from overcoming challenges. This provides a record of your growth journey and serves as a source of motivation during future difficulties.

Benefits of Seeking Lessons in Challenges:

1. Resilience Building: Viewing challenges as opportunities for growth contributes to the development of resilience. Individuals become better equipped to bounce back from setbacks and face future challenges with confidence.

2. Continuous Learning: Embracing challenges as learning opportunities fosters a mindset of continuous learning.

Individuals remain open to acquiring new knowledge and skills throughout their personal and professional journeys.

3. Adaptability: Challenges often require adaptability. By seeking lessons in difficult situations, individuals become more adaptable, learning to navigate change and uncertainty effectively.

4. Personal Development: Reframing challenges as opportunities for growth contributes to ongoing personal development. Individuals actively engage in self-improvement, honing skills and qualities that enhance their overall well-being.

5. Enhanced Problem-Solving Skills: Challenges provide a platform for honing problem-solving skills. By seeking solutions and learning from difficult situations, individuals enhance their ability to analyze problems and find effective resolutions.

Adapt to Your Preferences:

1. Collaborative Learning: Approach challenges as opportunities for collaborative learning. Seek input and perspectives from others, fostering a collective approach to overcoming difficulties.

2. Feedback Integration: Embrace feedback as a valuable source of learning during challenging situations. Solicit feedback from peers, mentors, or supervisors to gain insights that contribute to your growth.

3. Celebrate Small Wins: Acknowledge and celebrate small victories and milestones achieved during the challenge. Recognize the progress you make along the way, reinforcing a positive mindset.

4. Create a Growth Plan: Develop a growth plan that aligns with the challenges you face. Outline specific actions and learning goals that will contribute to your personal and professional development.
5. Connect with Mentors: Seek guidance from mentors or experienced individuals who have faced similar challenges. Their insights and advice can provide valuable perspectives and guidance for your growth journey.

By implementing this practical tool, individuals can navigate challenging situations with a constructive and growth-oriented mindset. Embracing difficulties as opportunities for learning not only enhances personal development but also contributes to a resilient and adaptive approach to life's challenges.

24) Seek Out Challenges:

Anecdote: Picture a mountain climber. The summit is rewarding because of the climb.

Interpretation: Challenges are opportunities for growth. Embrace them willingly rather than avoiding. Challenges foster resilience and personal development.

Practical Tool: Set deliberate challenges in your life, pushing beyond comfort zones. Embrace difficulties willingly, viewing them as stepping stones to improvement.

The practical tool involves intentionally setting challenges in your life, pushing beyond comfort zones, and willingly embracing difficulties as opportunities for improvement. This approach encourages individuals to proactively seek growth by confronting challenges that stretch their capabilities.

Setting Deliberate Challenges:

1. Identify Growth Areas: Reflect on areas of your life where you aspire to grow and improve. This could include personal development, career advancement, skill acquisition, or any aspect that aligns with your goals.

2. Define Specific Challenges: Clearly define specific challenges that align with your growth areas. These challenges should be measurable, realistic, and challenging enough to push you beyond your current comfort level.

Pushing Beyond Comfort Zones:

1. Recognize Comfort Zones: Identify the boundaries of your comfort zones. These are the areas where you feel at ease and familiar with the tasks or situations. Growth often occurs when you step beyond these zones.

2. Embrace Discomfort: Cultivate a mindset that embraces discomfort as a catalyst for growth. Understand that pushing beyond comfort zones is essential for expanding your capabilities and reaching new heights.

How to Implement the Tool:

1. Start with Incremental Challenges: Begin with challenges that are slightly beyond your current comfort level. Gradually increase the difficulty as you build confidence and resilience.

2. Create a Challenge Plan: Develop a plan for tackling deliberate challenges. Outline the steps, resources, and support needed to navigate each challenge successfully.

3. Establish Milestones: Break down larger challenges into smaller milestones. Setting achievable milestones provides a sense of progress and helps maintain motivation throughout the journey.
4. Seek Feedback: Actively seek feedback from mentors, peers, or experts who can provide insights and guidance during your challenges. Feedback contributes to continuous improvement.
5. Learn from Setbacks: Understand that setbacks are a natural part of taking on challenges. Instead of viewing setbacks as failures, see them as opportunities to learn and adjust your approach.

Benefits of Setting Deliberate Challenges:
1. Personal Growth and Development: Setting deliberate challenges promotes personal growth and development. It encourages individuals to acquire new skills, expand their knowledge, and develop a broader perspective.
2. Increased Resilience: Confronting challenges cultivates resilience. Individuals become better equipped to bounce back from setbacks and navigate uncertainties with a positive and adaptable mindset.
3. Expanded Comfort Zones: By willingly embracing difficulties, individuals expand their comfort zones. This leads to increased confidence and a willingness to tackle even more challenging tasks in the future.
4. Enhanced Problem-Solving Skills: Challenges stimulate problem-solving skills. Individuals learn to analyze situations, identify solutions, and adapt their strategies, contributing to enhanced problem-solving abilities.

5. Boosted Confidence: Successfully overcoming deliberate challenges boosts confidence. Individuals develop a sense of accomplishment and belief in their ability to handle future challenges.

Adapt to Your Preferences:

1. Align Challenges with Passion: Choose challenges that align with your passions and interests. This ensures that the efforts invested in overcoming challenges are personally rewarding.

2. Collaborate with Others: Collaborate with peers or form challenge groups where individuals collectively set and support each other in overcoming challenges. Shared experiences can provide valuable insights and motivation.

3. Balance Familiarity and Novelty: Strike a balance between challenges that are within your familiar domain and those that introduce novelty. This combination ensures a mix of comfort and growth opportunities.

4. Incorporate Reflection: Integrate reflective practices into your challenge journey. Regularly assess your experiences, learnings, and personal growth, adapting your approach based on insights gained.

5. Celebrate Achievements: Celebrate your achievements, both big and small, as you successfully navigate challenges. Acknowledge the progress made and use it as motivation for taking on new and more ambitious challenges.

By deliberately setting and embracing challenges, individuals can proactively shape their personal and professional growth. The intentional pursuit of difficulties fosters a mindset of continuous improvement and resilience, leading to a more fulfilling and impactful life.

25) Don't Follow the Mob:

Anecdote: Think of a school of fish. Choose your path deliberately instead of blindly following the crowd.

Interpretation: Individual conscience should guide actions, resisting conformity for virtue. Individuality often leads to more meaningful choices.

Practical Tool: Assess decisions independently, avoiding blindly following popular opinions. Reflect on decisions independently, considering your values rather than societal pressures.

The practical tool involves assessing decisions independently, steering clear of blindly following popular opinions. It emphasizes the importance of reflective decision-making, encouraging individuals to consider their values rather than succumbing to societal pressures.

Assessing Decisions Independently:

1. Cultivate Critical Thinking: Develop critical thinking skills to objectively analyze information, weigh pros and cons, and make informed decisions. This involves questioning assumptions, seeking evidence, and considering alternative perspectives.

2. Avoid Herd Mentality: Resist the urge to blindly follow popular opinions or conform to societal norms. Understand that what is popular or widely accepted may not always align with your unique values, goals, or circumstances.

Reflecting on Decisions Independently:

1. Understand Your Values: Clearly define and understand your personal values. These are the principles and beliefs that guide your life, influencing the decisions you make. Reflect on how a decision aligns with these values.
2. Consider Long-Term Impact: Reflect on the potential long-term impact of decisions. Consider how a choice today might affect your future well-being, goals, and overall satisfaction. This perspective helps in making decisions that are aligned with your aspirations.

How to Implement the Tool:

1. Pause and Reflect: Before making a decision, take a pause to reflect. Avoid making impulsive choices based on external pressures. Give yourself the time and space to think independently.
2. Evaluate Sources of Influence: Identify the sources of influence that may be shaping your opinions or decisions. Assess whether these influences are aligned with your values or if they are external pressures that may not serve your best interests.
3. Clarify Personal Goals: Clarify your personal goals and aspirations. Consider how a decision contributes to or hinders your progress towards these goals. This clarity helps in making decisions that align with your overarching objectives.
4. Seek Diverse Perspectives: Gather diverse perspectives on the decision at hand. Engage with individuals who offer different

viewpoints, allowing you to consider a range of opinions before arriving at an independent decision.

5. Be Mindful of Emotional Influences: Be mindful of emotional influences that may cloud your judgment. Emotions can impact decision-making, and it's essential to evaluate choices with a clear and rational mindset.

Benefits of Independent Decision-Making:

1. Authenticity: Independent decision-making fosters authenticity. Individuals make choices that genuinely reflect their values, leading to a more authentic and fulfilling life.

2. Personal Empowerment: Taking control of decisions empowers individuals to shape their own path. It instills a sense of personal responsibility and ownership over the outcomes of choices.

3. Alignment with Goals: Decisions made independently are more likely to align with personal goals and aspirations. This alignment contributes to a sense of purpose and direction in life.

4. Resilience: Developing the ability to make independent decisions builds resilience. Individuals become better equipped to navigate challenges and setbacks with confidence in their decision-making abilities.

5. Increased Self-Knowledge: Reflecting on decisions independently enhances self-knowledge. Individuals gain a deeper understanding of their values, preferences, and priorities through the decision-making process.

Adapt to Your Preferences:

1. Balance Input and Independence: Find a balance between seeking input from others and maintaining independence in

decision-making. Consider external perspectives while staying true to your values.

2. Continuous Learning: Embrace decisions as opportunities for continuous learning. Reflect on the outcomes of decisions, learn from experiences, and use insights to refine your decision-making process.

3. Encourage Constructive Criticism: Be open to constructive criticism and feedback. Constructive input can provide valuable insights that contribute to more informed and thoughtful decision-making.

4. Explore Unconventional Paths: Consider exploring unconventional or non-traditional paths when making decisions. Challenge societal norms if they conflict with your values and goals.

5. Regularly Reassess Values: Values may evolve over time. Regularly reassess and refine your values to ensure that your decisions remain aligned with your evolving sense of self and aspirations.

By incorporating this practical tool into your decision-making process, you empower yourself to make choices that are authentic, aligned with your values, and conducive to personal growth. Independent decision-making enhances self-awareness and resilience, contributing to a more intentional and fulfilling life journey.

26) Grab the "Smooth Handle":

Anecdote: Imagine a door. Choose the easiest path, removing unnecessary friction.

Interpretation: Interpret events positively. Shift focus to aspects within your control for peace of mind. Opt for simplicity in decision-making and actions.

Practical Tool: When faced with challenges, identify positive aspects or opportunities within them. When faced with choices, consider the path of least resistance without compromising values. The practical tool involves interpreting events positively, shifting focus to aspects within your control for peace of mind, and opting for simplicity in decision-making and actions. This approach encourages individuals to cultivate a positive mindset, prioritize elements they can influence, and simplify their decision-making processes.

Interpreting Events Positively:

1. Positive Framing: Practice positive framing by interpreting events in a constructive light. Instead of focusing on challenges or setbacks, look for opportunities for growth, learning, or positive outcomes.

2. Gratitude Practice: Cultivate a gratitude mindset by reflecting on the positive aspects of situations. Acknowledge and appreciate the good in your life, even during challenging times.

Shift Focus to Aspects Within Your Control:

1. Identify Controllable Factors: Identify factors within your control in any given situation. Recognize that while you may not control

external events, you have agency over your responses, choices, and attitudes.

2. Prioritize Energy: Direct your energy towards aspects you can influence rather than dwelling on those beyond your control. Prioritize actions that contribute to positive outcomes and personal well-being.

Opt for Simplicity in Decision-Making and Actions:

1. Simplify Decision-Making: Opt for simplicity in decision-making by focusing on essential factors. Avoid unnecessary complexity and overthinking. Streamline your choices by considering the most critical aspects.

2. Prioritize Key Actions: Identify key actions that align with your goals and values. Avoid overloading yourself with tasks and prioritize actions that contribute meaningfully to your objectives.

How to Implement the Tool:

1. Mindful Awareness: Practice mindful awareness to catch negative thoughts and reframe them positively. Cultivate an awareness of your thought patterns and consciously choose positive interpretations.

2. Control Assessment: Assess situations by distinguishing between factors you can control and those you cannot. Channel your focus and efforts towards actions that fall within your sphere of influence.

3. Simplicity Checklist: Before making decisions, create a simplicity checklist. Consider if the decision aligns with your values, if it's essential, and if there are simpler ways to achieve the desired outcome.

4. Positive Affirmations: Incorporate positive affirmations into your daily routine. Affirmations can reinforce a positive mindset and help shift your perspective towards a more optimistic view of events.

5. Mindfulness Meditation: Engage in mindfulness meditation to enhance your ability to stay present and focused. Mindfulness practices can contribute to a sense of calm and clarity in decision-making.

Benefits of Positive Interpretation, Focus, and Simplicity:

1. Emotional Well-being: Positive interpretation contributes to emotional well-being. Focusing on positive aspects and simplifying decision-making can reduce stress and promote a sense of peace.

2. Increased Resilience: A focus on controllable factors and positive framing enhances resilience. Individuals become better equipped to adapt to challenges and setbacks with a constructive mindset.

3. Improved Decision Quality: Simplifying decision-making allows for clearer thinking and improved decision quality. By focusing on essential factors, individuals can make more effective and efficient choices.

4. Enhanced Productivity: Prioritizing key actions and simplifying tasks enhances productivity. It allows individuals to focus their energy on impactful activities, leading to better outcomes.

5. Positive Relationships: A positive interpretation of events contributes to positive interactions in relationships. Simplifying decision-making can reduce unnecessary conflicts and promote understanding.

Adapt to Your Preferences:

1. Daily Positivity Journal: Maintain a daily positivity journal where you record positive events, gratitude, and lessons learned. Reflecting on positive aspects can reinforce a positive mindset.

2. Visualization Techniques: Use visualization techniques to imagine positive outcomes and successful actions. Visualization can contribute to a more optimistic outlook and boost confidence.

3. Delegate and Collaborate: Simplify tasks by delegating responsibilities and collaborating with others. Recognize when collective efforts can contribute to simpler and more effective solutions.

4. Regular Self-Reflection: Engage in regular self-reflection to assess your mindset, focus, and decision-making processes. Adjust your approach based on insights gained from self-reflection.

5. Experiment with Minimalism: Explore minimalist principles in various aspects of your life. Simplifying your environment and lifestyle can have positive effects on your mental clarity and overall well-being.

By incorporating this practical tool into your daily life, you can foster a positive mindset, enhance your ability to focus on controllable factors, and simplify your decision-making processes. These practices contribute to greater peace of mind, improved resilience, and a more intentional and fulfilling way of approaching life's challenges.

27) Every Person Is an Opportunity for Kindness (Seneca):

Anecdote: Picture a ripple effect. Kindness spreads, influencing others positively.

Interpretation: Cultivate kindness regardless of others' actions, contributing to a positive world. View interactions as chances to spread goodwill.

Practical Tool: Perform one act of kindness daily, whether a small gesture or a thoughtful word. Incorporate small acts of kindness into daily life, creating a positive impact.

The practical tool involves performing one act of kindness daily, whether a small gesture or a thoughtful word. This approach encourages individuals to incorporate small acts of kindness into their daily lives, creating a positive impact on both themselves and those around them.

Performing One Act of Kindness Daily:

1. Variety of Acts: Acts of kindness can take various forms, from simple gestures like holding the door for someone or offering a compliment to more significant acts like helping a neighbor or volunteering your time. The key is to make kindness a regular part of your routine.

2. Thoughtful Words: Kindness isn't limited to actions; it also includes the words we use. Offer words of encouragement, express gratitude, or provide support to others through your language.

Incorporating Small Acts of Kindness:

1. Daily Intention: Set a daily intention to perform at least one act of kindness. This intention serves as a reminder to actively seek opportunities to contribute positively to the lives of others.

2. Observation and Sensitivity: Be observant and sensitive to the needs and emotions of those around you. Kindness often involves recognizing when someone could use support or a positive interaction.

How to Implement the Tool:

1. Create a Kindness Calendar: Develop a kindness calendar where you plan specific acts of kindness for each day. This could include sending a kind message, helping a colleague, or performing random acts of kindness in your community.

2. Spontaneity and Genuine Gestures: Embrace spontaneity and let your acts of kindness arise naturally. Genuine gestures often have a more significant impact, and they don't necessarily need to be planned.

3. Reflect on Impact: Take a moment each day to reflect on the impact of your kindness. Consider how your actions may have brightened someone's day or positively influenced their well-being.

4. Encourage Others: Encourage others to join you in practicing daily acts of kindness. Create a positive ripple effect by inspiring those around you to incorporate kindness into their routines.

5. Document Your Kindness Journey: Keep a journal documenting your daily acts of kindness. Reflect on the experiences, emotions, and connections that arise from your kindness journey.

Benefits of Daily Acts of Kindness:

1. Enhanced Well-being: Engaging in acts of kindness has been linked to enhanced well-being. Both the giver and receiver experience positive emotions, contributing to overall life satisfaction.

2. Strengthened Connections: Kindness strengthens social connections. Regular acts of kindness create a sense of community and foster positive relationships with those around you.

3. Increased Positive Energy: Acts of kindness generate positive energy. They create a more positive and uplifting environment, not only for the recipients but also for the person performing the acts.

4. Cultivation of Empathy: Regular acts of kindness cultivate empathy. Individuals become more attuned to the emotions and needs of others, fostering a compassionate and understanding mindset.

5. Contribution to a Positive Culture: Consistent acts of kindness contribute to a positive culture in communities, workplaces, and families. They promote a supportive and uplifting atmosphere.

Adapt to Your Preferences:

1. Personalize Acts of Kindness: Tailor your acts of kindness to align with your personal strengths and interests. Whether it's

using your skills to help someone or offering a listening ear, personalize your approach.

2. Involve Others in Kindness Projects: Collaborate with friends, family, or colleagues on kindness projects. This could involve organizing group initiatives or challenges to collectively make a positive impact.

3. Connect Kindness to Personal Values: Align your acts of kindness with your personal values. Consider how your values can guide the type of kindness you choose to practice and the impact you aim to make.

4. Explore New Forms of Kindness: Continuously explore new forms of kindness. Challenge yourself to step outside your comfort zone and try different ways of contributing positively to the lives of others.

5. Extend Kindness to Yourself: Remember to extend kindness to yourself. Self-compassion is an essential aspect of overall well-being, so include acts of self-kindness in your daily practice.

By incorporating this practical tool into your daily routine, you contribute to a culture of kindness, empathy, and positivity. Regular acts of kindness have a cumulative effect, creating a more compassionate and supportive environment in your personal and social spheres.

28) Say No (A Lot):

Anecdote: Think of a packed suitcase. Saying no allows space for meaningful yeses.

Interpretation: Saying 'no' preserves time and energy for what truly matters, preventing burnout. Prioritize commitments; saying no protects your time and energy.

Practical Tool: Establish clear priorities and say 'no' to tasks that don't align with them. Assess the value of each request and decline when it doesn't align with your priorities.

The practical tool involves establishing clear priorities and being assertive in saying 'no' to tasks that don't align with those priorities. This approach emphasizes the importance of assessing the value of each request and declining those that do not contribute to your overarching goals.

Establishing Clear Priorities:

1. Define Core Values and Goals: Clearly define your core values and overarching goals. These could be related to your personal life, career, relationships, or any other area that holds significance for you.
2. Identify Key Priorities: Identify the key priorities that align with your values and goals. These are the tasks, projects, or activities that have the most significant impact on your overall well-being and success.

Saying 'No' to Tasks that Don't Align:

1. Assessing Value: When presented with a task or request, assess its value in relation to your priorities. Consider how it contributes to your goals and whether it aligns with your values.

2. Clarify Expectations: If unsure about the expectations or implications of a task, seek clarification before making a decision. Understanding the full scope of a request helps in evaluating its alignment with your priorities.

How to Implement the Tool:

1. Prioritize Tasks: Prioritize your tasks based on their alignment with your established priorities. Focus on high-priority activities that have a direct impact on your long-term goals.

2. Create a Criteria Checklist: Develop a criteria checklist for evaluating tasks. Consider factors such as relevance to your goals, time commitment, and overall alignment with your values. Use this checklist to guide your decision-making process.

3. Practice Assertiveness: Practice assertiveness in saying 'no.' Clearly communicate your decision and the reasons behind it. Be firm yet respectful in expressing that the task does not align with your current priorities.

4. Delegate When Appropriate: If the task is important but not aligned with your priorities, consider delegating it to someone better suited or available to handle it. Delegation is a valuable skill in effective time and resource management.

5. Set Boundaries: Establish and communicate clear boundaries. Let others know the limits of your time and availability. Setting boundaries helps manage expectations and prevents overwhelm.

Benefits of Establishing Clear Priorities and Saying 'No':

1. Focus and Productivity: Establishing clear priorities allows you to direct your energy toward tasks that truly matter. Saying 'no' to unrelated or less important tasks enhances focus and productivity.

2. Alignment with Goals: Saying 'no' to tasks that don't align with your priorities ensures that your actions are in alignment with your overarching goals. This contributes to a more purposeful and intentional life.

3. Reduced Overcommitment: Learning to say 'no' helps in avoiding overcommitment. By declining tasks that do not align with your priorities, you prevent spreading yourself too thin and maintain a healthy work-life balance.

4. Increased Effectiveness: Prioritizing tasks and declining irrelevant ones increases your overall effectiveness. It allows you to channel your efforts into activities that yield the greatest impact.

5. Improved Well-being: Saying 'no' to tasks that don't align with your priorities reduces stress and prevents burnout. It contributes to improved mental and emotional well-being by focusing on what truly matters.

Adapt to Your Preferences:

1. Periodic Priority Review: Conduct periodic reviews of your priorities to ensure they remain relevant. Adjust them as needed based on changes in your goals, values, or life circumstances.

2. Effective Communication Skills: Hone your communication skills to articulate your priorities and decisions clearly. Effective communication helps others understand your perspective and respect your choices.

3. Flexibility in Adjusting Priorities: Maintain a degree of flexibility in adjusting priorities when necessary. Life is dynamic, and being adaptable allows you to respond to changing circumstances without compromising your values.

4. Continuous Learning and Reflection: Engage in continuous learning and reflection to refine your understanding of what truly matters to you. Regular self-reflection contributes to a deeper awareness of your values and priorities.

5. Seek Support and Guidance: Seek support and guidance from mentors, colleagues, or friends. Discussing your priorities with others can provide valuable insights and alternative perspectives, helping you make more informed decisions.

By implementing this practical tool, individuals can enhance their ability to focus on what truly matters, aligning their actions with their core values and long-term goals. Saying 'no' assertively and strategically contributes to a more intentional and purpose-driven approach to life and work.

29) Don't Be Afraid to Ask for Help:

Anecdote: Picture a team of rowers. Asking for help propels you forward faster.

Interpretation: Seeking help is a strength. It fosters growth and shared wisdom. Strength lies in acknowledging when support is needed.

Practical Tool: Identify areas where you need support and proactively seek guidance. Overcome pride and seek assistance when facing challenges beyond your capacity.

The practical tool involves identifying areas where you need support and proactively seeking guidance. It emphasizes the importance of overcoming pride and being willing to seek assistance when facing challenges beyond your capacity.

Identifying Areas Needing Support:

1. Self-Awareness: Cultivate self-awareness to identify areas in which you may need support. This involves recognizing your strengths, weaknesses, and areas where additional knowledge or expertise could be beneficial.

2. Reflective Practices: Engage in reflective practices to assess your current skills and capabilities. Regular self-reflection helps you recognize where you may encounter challenges and where seeking support would be advantageous.

Proactively Seeking Guidance:

1. Initiate Communication: Take the initiative to communicate with others when you recognize a need for support. Actively seek

guidance by initiating conversations with mentors, colleagues, or individuals with relevant expertise.

2. Openness to Learning: Cultivate an openness to learning and a willingness to acknowledge that seeking guidance is a valuable part of personal and professional growth. Embrace the mindset that continuous learning involves reaching out for assistance when needed.

Overcoming Pride:

1. Embrace Humility: Embrace humility as a strength. Recognize that seeking support is not a sign of weakness but a demonstration of humility and a commitment to improvement.

2. Shift Perspective: Shift your perspective on asking for help. Instead of viewing it as a vulnerability, see it as a proactive step toward achieving success and overcoming challenges.

How to Implement the Tool:

1. Create a Support Network: Establish a support network of mentors, peers, or experts in relevant fields. Cultivate relationships with individuals who can offer guidance and support when needed.

2. Regular Check-Ins: Schedule regular check-ins with yourself to assess your progress and identify any challenges that may arise. Use these check-ins to determine when seeking guidance is necessary.

3. Build a Learning Plan: Develop a learning plan that includes seeking guidance in areas where you may lack expertise. Outline specific goals for knowledge acquisition and identify resources or individuals who can provide support.

4. Ask Direct Questions: When seeking guidance, ask direct and specific questions. Clearly communicate the areas in which you need support, making it easier for others to provide relevant and targeted advice.

5. Acknowledge Mistakes: Acknowledge mistakes or areas where you may have fallen short. Instead of allowing pride to hinder growth, use these instances as opportunities to learn and improve with the support of others.

Benefits of Proactively Seeking Guidance:

1. Accelerated Learning: Proactively seeking guidance accelerates the learning process. Learning from the experiences and insights of others allows you to gain knowledge more efficiently.

2. Enhanced Problem-Solving: Collaborating with others and seeking guidance enhances problem-solving capabilities. Different perspectives contribute to more comprehensive and effective solutions.

3. Personal and Professional Growth: Seeking guidance fosters personal and professional growth. It demonstrates a commitment to continuous improvement and a willingness to expand your skills and knowledge.

4. Strengthened Relationships: Building a support network and seeking guidance strengthens relationships. It creates a sense of collaboration and mutual support, fostering positive connections with mentors, colleagues, and peers.

5. Improved Decision-Making: Seeking guidance in decision-making ensures that choices are well-informed. Input from

experienced individuals can provide valuable insights that contribute to better decision outcomes.

Adapt to Your Preferences:

1. Utilize Online Resources: Explore online resources such as forums, webinars, and educational platforms as a means of seeking guidance. Virtual communities and platforms offer a wealth of knowledge and support.

2. Participate in Mentoring Programs: Engage in mentoring programs within your organization or industry. These programs provide structured opportunities to seek guidance and advice from experienced mentors.

3. Peer Collaboration: Foster a culture of peer collaboration where individuals support each other in overcoming challenges. Create an environment that encourages open communication and the sharing of knowledge among peers.

4. Feedback-Driven Improvement: View feedback as a catalyst for improvement. Actively seek feedback from others and use it as a guide for identifying areas where additional support or guidance may be beneficial.

5. Continuous Networking: Engage in continuous networking to expand your circle of contacts. Networking provides access to a diverse range of perspectives and expertise, enriching your ability to seek guidance when needed.

By implementing this practical tool, individuals can foster a proactive and open approach to seeking guidance. Overcoming pride and recognizing the value of collaborative learning contribute to personal and professional development, ultimately leading to more effective problem-solving and decision-making.

30) Find One Thing That Makes You Wiser Every Day:

Anecdote: Imagine a library. Each day, add a book of wisdom to your mental shelves.

Interpretation: Continuous learning enhances wisdom. Find lessons in daily experiences. Constant learning contributes to personal growth.

Practical Tool: Dedicate time each day to learn something new or gain a fresh perspective. Dedicate time daily to acquire new knowledge, fostering a curious mindset.

The practical tool involves dedicating time each day to learn something new or gain a fresh perspective. This approach encourages individuals to set aside specific time daily for acquiring new knowledge, fostering a curious mindset, and embracing continuous learning.

Dedicating Time for Daily Learning:

1. Time Allocation: Allocate a specific time each day dedicated to learning. Whether it's in the morning, during a lunch break, or in the evening, establishing a routine ensures consistency in daily learning efforts.

2. Curate Learning Resources: Curate a selection of learning resources that align with your interests, goals, or areas of curiosity. These resources can include books, articles, online courses, podcasts, videos, or any medium that facilitates learning.

Acquiring New Knowledge:

1. Explore Varied Topics: Explore a diverse range of topics to broaden your knowledge base. This diversity can contribute to a well-rounded understanding of various subjects and perspectives.

2. Set Learning Goals: Set specific learning goals for each session. Whether it's mastering a new skill, understanding a concept, or gaining insights into a particular industry, having clear objectives enhances the effectiveness of daily learning.

Fostering a Curious Mindset:

1. Ask Questions: Cultivate a habit of asking questions. In your daily interactions, encourage curiosity by seeking to understand concepts more deeply or exploring the "why" behind certain phenomena.

2. Embrace Challenges: Embrace challenges and view them as opportunities to learn. A curious mindset sees challenges as chances for growth and discovery rather than obstacles.

How to Implement the Tool:

1. Create a Learning Environment: Designate a specific space for learning that is conducive to focus and exploration. Whether it's a cozy reading nook, a quiet corner for online courses, or a dedicated desk, having a designated environment enhances the learning experience.

2. Utilize Technology: Leverage technology to access a wealth of learning materials. Explore educational apps, online platforms, and digital resources that cater to your interests. Technology provides convenient and diverse avenues for daily learning.

3. Mix Learning Formats: Mix learning formats to keep things engaging. Alternate between reading, watching videos, listening to podcasts, and participating in interactive online courses. Variety enhances the learning experience and caters to different learning preferences.
4. Share Insights: Share your newfound knowledge or insights with others. Engage in discussions, whether online or with friends and colleagues, to deepen your understanding and benefit from diverse perspectives.
5. Reflect on Learning: Take a few minutes each day to reflect on what you've learned. Consider how the new knowledge can be applied in different contexts or integrated into your personal or professional life.

Benefits of Daily Learning:

1. Continuous Personal Growth: Daily learning contributes to continuous personal growth. It ensures that you are constantly expanding your skills, knowledge, and perspectives, fostering a dynamic and evolving self.
2. Adaptability: Regular learning enhances adaptability. A curious mindset and a commitment to daily learning equip you with the skills and insights needed to navigate and adapt to a rapidly changing world.
3. Improved Problem-Solving: Acquiring diverse knowledge and perspectives enhances problem-solving abilities. Exposure to various concepts and ideas provides a rich toolkit for approaching challenges with creativity and innovation.

4. Professional Development: Continuous learning is a cornerstone of professional development. It keeps you relevant in your field, opens up new opportunities, and positions you as a lifelong learner, a quality highly valued in various industries.

5. Enhanced Creativity: Daily learning stimulates creativity. Exposure to different disciplines and ideas sparks creative thinking, leading to innovative solutions and a more imaginative approach to various aspects of life.

Adapt to Your Preferences:

1. Themed Learning Days: Designate themed learning days where each day is dedicated to a specific topic or subject. This structured approach adds variety to your daily learning routine.

2. Learning Buddies: Partner with learning buddies or study groups. Sharing the learning experience with others not only makes it more enjoyable but also provides opportunities for collaborative exploration.

3. Incorporate Physical Activity: Combine learning with physical activity. Listen to educational podcasts while going for a walk or engage in light exercises while watching educational videos. This integration enhances overall well-being.

4. Experiment with Learning Styles: Experiment with different learning styles to discover what works best for you. Whether it's visual learning, auditory learning, or hands-on experiences, tailor your daily learning activities to suit your preferred style.

5. Document Learning Journey: Keep a learning journal to document your daily discoveries, insights, and reflections. This

journal serves as a record of your learning journey and provides a resource for future reference.

By implementing this practical tool, individuals can cultivate a habit of continuous learning, nurturing a curious mindset that contributes to personal and professional development. Daily learning becomes a source of inspiration, growth, and a deeper understanding of the world.

31) What's Bad for the Hive Is Bad for the Bee (Marcus Aurelius):

Anecdote: Picture a beehive. The health of the individual depends on the well-being of the community.

Interpretation: Personal actions impact the whole. Foster harmony by considering the greater good. Individual actions impact the collective; consider the greater good.

Practical Tool: Reflect on how your actions contribute to the well-being of your community. Make choices mindful of their broader impact on your community.

The practical tool involves reflecting on how your actions contribute to the well-being of your community and making choices mindful of their broader impact. This approach encourages individuals to consider the consequences of their actions on the community and strive to make choices that positively contribute to communal well-being.

Reflecting on Community Impact:

1. Awareness of Interconnectedness: Develop an awareness of the interconnectedness of individuals within a community.

Recognize that actions, whether small or large, can have ripple effects on the well-being of the entire community.

2. Consideration of Stakeholders: Reflect on the diverse stakeholders in your community, including neighbors, local businesses, organizations, and the environment. Consider how your choices may affect these stakeholders and the broader community fabric.

Mindful Decision-Making:

1. Conscious Choices: Make conscious and deliberate choices in your daily life. Before taking actions, consider the potential impact on the community and choose options that align with the well-being and values of the collective.

2. Community-Centric Values: Cultivate community-centric values such as cooperation, empathy, and social responsibility. Prioritize choices that reflect these values, contributing to a positive community environment.

How to Implement the Tool:

1. Community Engagement: Engage actively in community activities and initiatives. Attend local events, participate in neighborhood clean-ups, and collaborate with community members to understand their needs and concerns.

2. Stay Informed: Stay informed about local issues, policies, and developments. Knowledge about the community's challenges and strengths empowers you to make informed choices that positively impact its well-being.

3. Collaborate with Others: Collaborate with community members on projects or initiatives that enhance well-being. Collective

efforts often yield more significant and sustainable positive outcomes for the community.

4. Support Local Businesses: Prioritize supporting local businesses and establishments. Choosing local products and services contributes to the economic vitality of the community and fosters a sense of unity.

5. Environmental Considerations: Consider the environmental impact of your actions. Make eco-friendly choices that contribute to the sustainability of local ecosystems and reduce the community's overall ecological footprint.

Benefits of Community-Centric Choices:

1. Strengthened Social Fabric: Mindful choices contribute to a strengthened social fabric. Prioritizing community well-being fosters a sense of unity and connectedness among residents.

2. Enhanced Quality of Life: Community-centric decisions often lead to an improved quality of life for residents. Choices that prioritize safety, inclusivity, and access to resources contribute to a thriving community.

3. Positive Community Dynamics: Mindful decision-making positively influences community dynamics. It encourages a culture of mutual support, cooperation, and shared responsibility, creating a more positive and harmonious community environment.

4. Increased Resilience: A community that makes choices mindful of its well-being is more resilient in the face of challenges. Collaboration and collective problem-solving become integral components of community resilience.

5. Environmental Sustainability: Considering the environmental impact of choices contributes to the long-term sustainability of the community. Environmental stewardship ensures that natural resources are preserved for future generations.

Adapt to Your Preferences:

1. Create Community Initiatives: Take the initiative to create or participate in community projects that address specific needs. This hands-on approach allows you to directly contribute to the well-being of your community.

2. Educate and Advocate: Educate yourself and others about community issues. Advocate for positive change by raising awareness and working towards solutions that benefit the community as a whole.

3. Encourage Inclusivity: Promote inclusivity within the community. Ensure that your choices contribute to an inclusive environment where diverse voices are heard and everyone feels a sense of belonging.

4. Volunteer Your Time: Dedicate time to volunteer for community organizations or events. Volunteering is a direct and impactful way to contribute to the well-being of your community.

5. Sustainable Living Practices: Embrace sustainable living practices in your daily life. This could include reducing waste, conserving energy, and supporting initiatives that promote environmental sustainability within the community.

By implementing this practical tool, individuals can actively contribute to the well-being of their community. Reflecting on the broader impact of choices fosters a sense of social responsibility and encourages actions that create a positive, resilient, and thriving community environment.

32) Don't Judge Other People:

Anecdote: Imagine a novel. People are complex characters with stories you may not fully understand.

Interpretation: Avoiding judgment fosters empathy, recognizing everyone's unique struggles. Avoid quick judgments; everyone has their journey.

Practical Tool: Challenge judgments by seeking to understand others' perspectives before forming opinions. Cultivate empathy, seeking to understand before passing judgment.

The practical tool involves challenging judgments by seeking to understand others' perspectives before forming opinions. It emphasizes the importance of cultivating empathy and adopting a mindset of seeking understanding before passing judgment.

Challenging Judgments:

1. Awareness of Judgments: Develop self-awareness to recognize when judgments arise. Acknowledge that everyone has biases and preconceptions, and the first step in challenging judgments is being aware of them.
2. Pause and Reflect: Before forming opinions or passing judgment, pause and take a moment to reflect on your initial thoughts. Consider whether your judgments are based on assumptions or limited information.

Seeking to Understand:

1. Empathetic Inquiry: Engage in empathetic inquiry by seeking to understand others' perspectives. Approach conversations with a genuine curiosity, asking questions to gain insight into their experiences, values, and motivations.

2. Active Listening: Practice active listening when engaging with others. Give them your full attention, avoid interrupting, and genuinely listen to their words, tone, and body language to understand the nuances of their perspective.

Cultivating Empathy:

1. Put Yourself in Their Shoes: Cultivate empathy by putting yourself in the shoes of others. Imagine what it's like to experience life from their perspective, considering their challenges, joys, and the context that shapes their views.

2. Open-Mindedness: Foster an open-minded attitude. Be receptive to different viewpoints, even if they challenge your existing beliefs. An open mind allows for the exploration of diverse perspectives without immediate judgment.

How to Implement the Tool:

1. Ask Clarifying Questions: When faced with opinions or statements that trigger judgments, ask clarifying questions. Seek additional information to understand the context and motivations behind the expressed views.

2. Engage in Perspective-Taking: Actively engage in perspective-taking exercises. Imagine how a situation might look from

someone else's point of view, considering their background, experiences, and emotions.

3. Diversify Information Sources: Diversify your information sources to gain a broader understanding of different perspectives. Exposure to diverse viewpoints helps challenge stereotypes and promotes a more nuanced understanding of complex issues.

4. Practice Reflective Journaling: Keep a reflective journal where you explore your own judgments and the process of seeking to understand others. Documenting your thoughts and experiences enhances self-awareness and reinforces the importance of empathy.

5. Engage in Empathy-Building Activities: Participate in activities that build empathy, such as volunteering, attending cultural events, or joining discussions with individuals from diverse backgrounds. These experiences provide opportunities to learn and connect on a human level.

Benefits of Challenging Judgments and Cultivating Empathy:

1. Improved Relationships: Challenging judgments and practicing empathy contribute to improved relationships. Understanding others fosters deeper connections and enhances communication and collaboration.

2. Conflict Resolution: Empathy is a key element in conflict resolution. By seeking to understand others' perspectives, individuals can find common ground, leading to more effective resolution of conflicts and misunderstandings.

3. Cultural Competence: Cultivating empathy contributes to cultural competence. Understanding and appreciating diverse

perspectives foster a more inclusive and harmonious environment in multicultural settings.

4. Enhanced Decision-Making: Challenging judgments leads to more informed decision-making. Considering a variety of perspectives allows for a comprehensive analysis of situations, leading to more thoughtful and inclusive decisions.

5. Personal Growth: Actively working to understand others and challenging judgments contributes to personal growth. It expands one's worldview, challenges biases, and encourages continuous self-reflection and improvement.

Adapt to Your Preferences:

1. Practice Mindfulness: Integrate mindfulness practices into your routine. Mindfulness enhances awareness of thoughts and judgments, providing an opportunity to pause and choose a more empathetic response.

2. Diversity of Conversations: Engage in conversations with a diverse range of people. Actively seek out perspectives that differ from your own, and use these interactions as opportunities to practice empathy and understanding.

3. Seek Feedback: Seek feedback from others about your communication style and openness to different perspectives. Valuable insights from those around you can guide your efforts to challenge judgments and cultivate empathy.

4. Read Widely: Expand your reading list to include a variety of authors, genres, and perspectives. Exposure to diverse literature enhances your ability to understand different viewpoints and challenges preconceived notions.

5. Join Empathy-Building Programs: Explore empathy-building programs or workshops in your community or online. Participating in structured programs can provide guidance and practical tools for developing and strengthening empathetic skills.

By implementing this practical tool, individuals can contribute to creating a more empathetic and understanding society. Challenging judgments and seeking to understand others foster a culture of inclusivity, compassion, and open-mindedness, ultimately leading to stronger connections and positive social dynamics.

33) Study the Lives of the Greats:

Anecdote: Picture a mentorship journey. Learning from the experiences of great individuals can guide your path.

Interpretation: Learning from exemplary figures provides guidance on virtues and overcoming challenges. Gain wisdom from the successes and failures of those who came before you.

Practical Tool: Read biographies or autobiographies of inspirational figures regularly and study the lives of accomplished individuals for inspiration.

The practical tool involves regularly reading biographies or autobiographies of inspirational figures and studying the lives of accomplished individuals for inspiration. This approach encourages individuals to learn from the experiences, challenges, and successes of notable personalities, gaining insights that can be applied to their own lives.

Regular Reading of Biographies:

1. Source of Inspiration: Biographies and autobiographies offer a rich source of inspiration. They provide narratives of individuals who have overcome challenges, achieved remarkable success, and made significant contributions to their fields or society.

2. Diverse Perspectives: Reading about a variety of individuals from different backgrounds, professions, and time periods exposes readers to diverse perspectives. This diversity of experiences allows for a well-rounded understanding of the human journey.

Studying Accomplished Individuals:

1. Analyzing Life Journeys: Studying the lives of accomplished individuals involves a deep analysis of their life journeys. This includes understanding their early influences, major life events, decision-making processes, and the strategies they employed to overcome obstacles.

2. Extracting Lessons and Principles: Extracting lessons and principles from the lives of accomplished individuals is a key aspect. Readers can identify patterns, values, and habits that contributed to the success of these individuals, applying these insights to their own lives.

How to Implement the Tool:

1. Curate a Diverse Reading List: Curate a diverse reading list that includes biographies and autobiographies from various fields such as business, science, arts, politics, and sports. Explore the lives of figures who resonate with your interests and aspirations.

2. Set a Reading Routine: Set a regular reading routine to incorporate biographies into your schedule. Whether it's a few pages each night or dedicated reading sessions, consistency allows for a continuous flow of inspiration and learning.
3. Take Notes and Reflect: Take notes while reading and reflect on key insights from each biography. Consider how the experiences of the individual relate to your own life, challenges, and goals. Note any lessons or principles that stand out.
4. Discuss with Others: Engage in discussions with others who have read the same biographies or share your insights with friends, family, or book clubs. Discussing the lives of accomplished individuals can provide additional perspectives and deepen your understanding.
5. Apply Lessons in Real Life: Actively apply the lessons learned from biographies in real-life situations. Implementing principles derived from inspirational figures can contribute to personal growth, decision-making, and the pursuit of goals.

Benefits of Reading Biographies for Inspiration:

1. Motivation and Resilience: Biographies often highlight the resilience and determination of individuals in the face of challenges. Reading about their perseverance can motivate and inspire readers to overcome their own obstacles.
2. Broadened Perspective: Exposure to a variety of life stories broadens one's perspective. Learning about individuals from different cultures, backgrounds, and professions fosters a more inclusive worldview.

3. Understanding Leadership Styles: Studying the lives of accomplished leaders provides insights into different leadership styles. Readers can learn about effective decision-making, team-building, and strategies for navigating complex situations.

4. Learning from Mistakes: Biographies often include accounts of mistakes and failures. Understanding how successful individuals rebounded from setbacks offers valuable lessons in resilience and learning from adversity.

5. Personal Development: Reading biographies contributes to personal development. It prompts self-reflection, encourages the setting of personal goals, and provides a roadmap for continuous improvement.

Adapt to Your Preferences:

1. Focus on Specific Themes: Tailor your reading list to focus on specific themes or qualities you want to develop. If you're interested in leadership, choose biographies of influential leaders. If resilience is a priority, explore stories of individuals who overcame significant challenges.

2. Combine Biographies with Other Genres: Combine biographies with other genres such as self-help, philosophy, or fiction. This diverse reading approach provides a well-rounded understanding of human experiences and perspectives.

3. Explore Autobiographical Essays: Explore autobiographical essays or collections of personal reflections. These shorter pieces offer glimpses into the thoughts, philosophies, and life experiences of individuals in a condensed format.

4. Create a Reading Journal: Maintain a reading journal where you document your reflections, favorite quotes, and key takeaways from each biography. Reviewing your journal over time provides a record of your personal growth and the wisdom gained.

5. Pair with Documentaries or Films: Enhance your understanding by pairing biographies with documentaries or films about the same individuals. Visual portrayals can provide additional insights into their lives and achievements.

By implementing this practical tool, individuals can draw inspiration from the lives of accomplished figures, gaining valuable insights to apply to their own journeys. Reading biographies becomes a continuous source of motivation, guidance, and learning that contributes to personal and professional development.

34) Forgive, Forgive, Forgive:

Anecdote: Visualize carrying a heavy burden. Forgiveness is the key to unburdening yourself.

Interpretation: Forgiveness liberates the self. Holding grudges only hinders personal growth.

Practical Tool: Practice forgiveness, understanding it is for your peace, not the wrongdoer's benefit. Practice forgiveness as a gift to yourself, letting go of resentment.

The practical tool involves practicing forgiveness as a gift to oneself, understanding that it is for personal peace rather than the benefit of the wrongdoer. It emphasizes the importance of letting go of resentment and embracing forgiveness as a means of achieving inner peace.

Understanding Forgiveness:

1. Release of Resentment: Forgiveness involves releasing resentment and negative emotions associated with a perceived wrongdoing. It is a conscious decision to free oneself from the emotional burden of holding onto anger, hurt, or grudges.

2. Self-Liberation: Forgiveness is a form of self-liberation. By choosing to forgive, individuals unshackle themselves from the chains of negative emotions, allowing for personal growth and the pursuit of inner peace.

Practicing Forgiveness for Personal Peace:

1. Shift in Perspective: Forgiveness involves a shift in perspective. Rather than focusing on the wrongdoer's actions, it centers on one's own well-being. The practice of forgiveness is a gift to oneself, aiming for internal harmony and tranquility.

2. Letting Go of Control: Forgiveness is a conscious choice to let go of the desire for control over past events. It acknowledges that one cannot change the past but can control their response to it. This relinquishing of control contributes to emotional freedom.

How to Implement the Tool:

1. Reflect on the Impact: Reflect on how holding onto resentment impacts your emotional well-being. Acknowledge the weight it adds to your life and consider forgiveness as a means of lightening that load.

2. Acknowledge Feelings: Acknowledge and validate your feelings of hurt or anger. Understanding and accepting these emotions is a crucial step before moving towards forgiveness.

3. Practice Empathy: Practice empathy by attempting to understand the perspective of the person who wronged you. Recognize that individuals are complex, and their actions may be influenced by various factors.
4. Separate the Person from the Action: Separate the person from their actions. Understand that people can make mistakes or act in hurtful ways, but those actions do not define their entire identity.
5. Choose to Forgive: Forgiveness is a conscious choice. Choose to forgive not as a favor to the wrongdoer but as a gift to yourself. Recognize that holding onto resentment only perpetuates your own suffering.
6. Establish Boundaries: Forgiveness doesn't necessarily mean condoning or forgetting the actions. It can coexist with the establishment of healthy boundaries to protect oneself from future harm.

Benefits of Practicing Forgiveness:

1. Inner Peace: The primary benefit of forgiveness is inner peace. Letting go of resentment and negative emotions contributes to a sense of calm and tranquility within oneself.
2. Emotional Healing: Forgiveness facilitates emotional healing. It allows individuals to process and release pent-up emotions, paving the way for healing from past wounds.
3. Improved Mental Health: Forgiveness is linked to improved mental health. It reduces stress, anxiety, and symptoms of depression, fostering a positive and resilient mindset.
4. Enhanced Relationships: Practicing forgiveness positively influences relationships. It creates a space for understanding,

empathy, and the rebuilding of trust, leading to healthier connections with others.

5. Personal Growth: Forgiveness is a catalyst for personal growth. It prompts self-reflection, resilience, and a commitment to positive change, fostering an environment for continuous self-improvement.

Adapt to Your Preferences:

1. Seek Support: Seek support from friends, family, or a counselor as you navigate the journey of forgiveness. Talking about your feelings and experiences can provide valuable insights and emotional support.

2. Express Your Feelings: Express your feelings through writing or other creative outlets. Articulating your emotions can be a cathartic process and may aid in the forgiveness journey.

3. Explore Mindfulness Practices: Integrate mindfulness practices into your routine. Mindfulness meditation and awareness exercises can enhance your ability to stay present and let go of lingering negative emotions.

4. Engage in Self-Care: Prioritize self-care activities that promote overall well-being. Physical exercise, relaxation techniques, and activities that bring joy contribute to a positive mindset conducive to forgiveness.

5. Educate Yourself: Read books or attend workshops on forgiveness and personal growth. Educating yourself about the psychological and emotional aspects of forgiveness can provide valuable insights and tools for practice.

By implementing this practical tool, individuals can experience the transformative power of forgiveness. Choosing to forgive as a gift to oneself allows for the cultivation of inner peace, emotional healing, and personal growth, fostering a positive and fulfilling life journey.

35) Make a Little Progress Each Day:

Anecdote: Picture a journey. Consistent small steps lead to significant distances covered.

Interpretation: Consistent effort leads to significant growth over time. Focus on small daily advancements. Incremental progress is sustainable and adds up over time.

Practical Tool: Set achievable daily goals, celebrating small wins and progress. Set achievable daily goals, focusing on gradual improvement.

The practical tool involves setting achievable daily goals, celebrating small wins, and focusing on gradual improvement. This approach emphasizes the importance of breaking down larger objectives into manageable tasks, acknowledging and celebrating small successes, and fostering a mindset of continuous progress.

Setting Achievable Daily Goals:

1. Define Clear Objectives: Clearly define the objectives you want to achieve. Break down larger goals into smaller, actionable tasks that can be realistically accomplished within a day.

2. Prioritize Tasks: Prioritize tasks based on urgency, importance, or impact. Identify the key activities that align with your overall goals and focus on those as your primary daily goals.

Celebrating Small Wins:

1. Acknowledge Achievements: Acknowledge and celebrate small achievements throughout the day. Recognize the completion of tasks, no matter how minor, as valuable steps toward your larger goals.

2. Positive Reinforcement: Use positive reinforcement to motivate yourself. Celebrate small wins with positive affirmations, a mental pat on the back, or a small reward to create a positive association with goal achievement.

Focusing on Gradual Improvement:

1. Continuous Learning: Embrace a mindset of continuous learning and improvement. View each day as an opportunity to learn, grow, and refine your skills, recognizing that progress often happens incrementally.

2. Adapt and Adjust: Be flexible in your approach and willing to adapt. If you encounter challenges or unexpected obstacles, consider them learning opportunities and adjust your goals accordingly for the day.

How to Implement the Tool:

1. Set Daily Intentions: Begin each day by setting clear intentions for what you want to achieve. Identify the specific tasks or activities that, when completed, will contribute to your overall goals.

2. Break Down Larger Goals: Break down larger, long-term goals into smaller, manageable steps. This makes the goals more achievable and provides a roadmap for daily actions.

3. Use a Task Management System: Utilize a task management system, whether it's a to-do list, a digital productivity tool, or a planner. Organize your daily goals, prioritize tasks, and track your progress.

4. Regularly Assess Progress: Regularly assess your progress throughout the day. Take brief moments to reflect on what you've accomplished, what's remaining, and if any adjustments to your goals are needed.

5. Celebrate Milestones: Celebrate not only the completion of daily goals but also significant milestones in your larger objectives. This could involve more substantial rewards or recognition for achieving certain levels of progress.

Benefits of Setting Achievable Daily Goals:

1. Motivation and Momentum: Setting and achieving daily goals provides a sense of motivation and builds momentum. Small successes create a positive cycle of accomplishment and drive.

2. Increased Productivity: Breaking down tasks into achievable goals increases overall productivity. It helps maintain focus and prevents feeling overwhelmed by large, complex objectives.

3. Positive Mindset: Celebrating small wins fosters a positive mindset. A positive outlook enhances resilience, optimism, and a willingness to tackle new challenges.

4. Continuous Progress: Focusing on gradual improvement ensures continuous progress. It encourages a consistent effort toward goals, even on days when tasks may seem less significant.

5. Reduced Stress: Breaking down goals into manageable daily tasks can reduce stress. It provides a structured approach,

allowing you to focus on one step at a time rather than feeling overwhelmed by the larger picture.

Adapt to Your Preferences:

1. Time Blocking: Implement time blocking to allocate specific time periods for different tasks. This structured approach helps manage your schedule and ensures dedicated time for goal-related activities.

2. Include Personal Development Goals: Integrate personal development goals into your daily plan. This could include activities like reading, learning a new skill, or practicing mindfulness, contributing to holistic growth.

3. Collaborate with Accountability Partners: Partner with friends, colleagues, or mentors as accountability partners. Share your daily goals with them, and mutually celebrate achievements. Accountability partnerships can provide support and encouragement.

4. Review and Adjust Weekly: Conduct a weekly review to assess your progress, celebrate weekly achievements, and adjust goals for the upcoming week. This practice ensures ongoing alignment with your overall objectives.

5. Experiment with Daily Themes: Experiment with daily themes where each day is dedicated to a specific aspect of your goals. For example, one day could focus on learning, another on productivity, and another on self-care.

By implementing this practical tool, individuals can create a framework for consistent progress, motivation, and a positive mindset. Setting achievable daily goals, celebrating small wins, and focusing on gradual improvement contribute to long-term success and personal fulfillment.

36) Journal:

Anecdote: Imagine a conversation with your past self. Journaling is a dialogue with your thoughts.

Interpretation: Journaling enhances self-awareness, serving as a tool for reflection and personal growth. Writing clarifies your thoughts and provides a record of your journey.

Practical Tool: Maintain a journal to record thoughts, experiences, and lessons learned. Regularly journal to reflect on experiences, emotions, and personal growth.

The practical tool involves maintaining a journal to record thoughts, experiences, and lessons learned. The practice of regularly journaling allows individuals to reflect on their experiences, emotions, and personal growth.

Maintaining a Journal:

1. Capture Thoughts and Experiences: A journal serves as a personal space to capture thoughts, experiences, and observations. It provides a medium for expressing feelings, recording memories, and documenting the details of daily life.

2. Versatility of Content: Journals are versatile and can include a wide range of content such as reflections, anecdotes, goals, dreams, challenges, and achievements. This flexibility allows individuals to tailor their journaling practice to suit their preferences.

Regularly Journaling for Reflection:

1. Emotional Release: Regular journaling provides a channel for emotional release. It allows individuals to express and process emotions, leading to a greater understanding of their feelings and contributing to emotional well-being.

2. Reflection on Experiences: Journaling offers a space for reflecting on experiences. By revisiting past entries, individuals can gain insights into patterns, identify recurring themes, and understand the impact of various events on their lives.

3. Tracking Personal Growth: Documenting thoughts and experiences over time enables individuals to track their personal growth. Reviewing past entries reveals progress, changes in perspectives, and the evolution of values and priorities.

4. Lessons Learned: Journals serve as repositories of lessons learned. By reflecting on challenges and successes, individuals can distill valuable insights and wisdom that contribute to ongoing learning and development.

5. Clarity and Self-Discovery: Journaling promotes clarity of thought and self-discovery. Through the process of putting thoughts into words, individuals gain a deeper understanding of themselves, their motivations, and the factors influencing their decisions.

How to Implement the Tool:

1. Choose a Journaling Medium: Choose a journaling medium that suits your preferences. This could be a physical notebook, a

digital journaling app, or even a combination of both. Select a format that feels comfortable and accessible.

2. Establish a Routine: Set aside dedicated time for journaling. Whether it's in the morning, evening, or during specific life events, establishing a routine helps integrate journaling into your daily or weekly activities.

3. Write Freely: Write freely without judgment. Allow your thoughts to flow without worrying about grammar or structure. The aim is to express yourself authentically and capture the essence of your experiences.

4. Experiment with Prompts: Experiment with journaling prompts to spark creativity and self-reflection. Prompts can be specific questions, open-ended statements, or themes that guide your writing and encourage deeper exploration.

5. Include Gratitude Practice: Integrate gratitude into your journaling practice. Regularly expressing gratitude can shift focus to positive aspects of life, fostering a more optimistic outlook and enhancing overall well-being.

Benefits of Regular Journaling:

1. Improved Mental Health: Journaling is associated with improved mental health. It provides an outlet for managing stress, processing emotions, and gaining perspective on challenging situations.

2. Enhanced Self-Awareness: Regular journaling enhances self-awareness. It encourages introspection, helping individuals understand their values, strengths, weaknesses, and areas for personal development.

3. Documenting Progress: Journaling serves as a documented timeline of personal progress. Tracking achievements, challenges, and milestones provides a tangible record of growth over time.

4. Increased Clarity: Writing about thoughts and experiences fosters increased clarity of thought. It helps individuals articulate their feelings, leading to a better understanding of themselves and their motivations.

5. Stress Reduction: The act of journaling can be a stress-reducing activity. Writing about concerns, fears, or anxieties can provide a sense of release and contribute to a more balanced mental state.

Adapt to Your Preferences:

1. Visual Journaling: Explore visual journaling by incorporating sketches, drawings, or collages alongside written entries. Visual elements can add another layer of expression and creativity to the journaling process.

2. Digital Journaling Apps: Embrace digital journaling apps that offer features such as multimedia integration, password protection, and the ability to sync across devices. Digital platforms can enhance accessibility and organization.

3. Themed Journals: Experiment with themed journals focused on specific aspects of your life, such as gratitude, personal goals, or daily reflections. Themed journals provide structure and purpose to your writing.

4. Share or Keep Private: Decide whether you want to keep your journal private or share selected insights with others. Some

individuals find value in sharing their thoughts, while others prefer to keep their journals personal.

5. Include Future Goals: Include future goals and aspirations in your journal. Regularly revisiting these entries can serve as a source of motivation and a reminder of the direction you want to move toward.

By implementing this practical tool, individuals can harness the benefits of regular journaling for self-reflection, personal growth, and emotional well-being. The practice becomes a valuable tool for understanding oneself, navigating life's challenges, and cultivating a positive and mindful approach to daily living.

37) Prepare for Life's Inevitable Setbacks (Premeditatio Malorum):

Anecdote: Picture a chess game. Anticipating setbacks is like planning your moves ahead.

Interpretation: Anticipating challenges mentally equips us to face them with stoic fortitude. Mental preparation cushions the impact of life's challenges.

Practical Tool: Regularly engage in a mental exercise envisioning potential challenges and your response. Visualize potential obstacles and plan your response in advance.

The practical tool involves regularly engaging in a mental exercise where you envision potential challenges and plan your response in advance. This proactive approach helps individuals prepare for obstacles, cultivate resilience, and develop effective strategies for overcoming difficulties.

Regular Mental Exercise:

1. Envisioning Potential Challenges: Set aside time regularly to engage in a mental exercise where you envision potential challenges that may arise in different areas of your life. This could include challenges at work, in relationships, personal goals, or any other relevant aspect.

2. Anticipating Various Scenarios: Anticipate various scenarios and potential obstacles. Consider both internal challenges (such as self-doubt or fear) and external challenges (such as unexpected setbacks or conflicts). This comprehensive approach allows for a more thorough mental preparation.

Planning Your Response:

1. Strategic Planning: As you visualize potential challenges, engage in strategic planning for your response. Consider different strategies, solutions, and coping mechanisms that align with your goals and values.

2. Identifying Resources: Identify internal and external resources that can support you in overcoming challenges. This could include your strengths, skills, support networks, or external tools and information.

3. Cultivating Resilience: Focus on cultivating resilience by envisioning not only the challenges but also the potential for growth and learning that may come from overcoming them. Embrace a mindset that views challenges as opportunities for personal development.

4. Stress Testing Plans: Stress test your plans by considering potential obstacles or complications that may arise during the execution of your strategies. This iterative process helps refine your responses and ensures adaptability in dynamic situations.

How to Implement the Tool:

1. Set a Regular Schedule: Dedicate specific times in your routine to engage in this mental exercise. It could be a weekly or monthly practice, allowing you to maintain a proactive mindset without feeling overwhelmed.

2. Create a Quiet Environment: Choose a quiet and comfortable environment for this exercise. Minimize distractions to fully immerse yourself in the mental process of envisioning challenges and planning your responses.

3. Visualize in Detail: Visualize challenges in detail, imagining the specific scenarios, emotions, and potential roadblocks. The more vividly you can picture these challenges, the better prepared you'll be in real-life situations.

4. Document Your Plans: Document your plans and responses. This could be in the form of written notes, a digital document, or a journal. Documenting your thoughts helps reinforce the mental exercise and provides a reference when needed.

5. Revisit and Revise: Regularly revisit and revise your plans. As circumstances and goals evolve, so should your responses to potential challenges. This ongoing reflection ensures that your strategies remain relevant and effective.

Benefits of Regularly Envisioning Challenges:

1. Increased Preparedness: Regularly envisioning challenges enhances your preparedness for unexpected situations. This proactive mindset allows you to respond more calmly and confidently when faced with obstacles.

2. Improved Decision-Making: The mental exercise of planning your response contributes to improved decision-making. It allows you to consider multiple options, weigh their pros and cons, and choose the most effective course of action.

3. Stress Reduction: Anticipating challenges in a controlled mental space reduces the element of surprise and potential stress. You approach challenges with a sense of readiness, minimizing the impact on your overall well-being.

4. Enhanced Adaptability: Envisioning potential challenges and planning responses enhances your adaptability. By thinking through various scenarios, you become more flexible in adjusting your strategies to fit the specific circumstances.

5. Confidence Building: Proactively planning for challenges builds confidence in your ability to navigate difficult situations. This sense of confidence positively influences your mindset and resilience when faced with real challenges.

Adapt to Your Preferences:

1. Visualization Techniques: Explore different visualization techniques to make the mental exercise more effective. This could include guided imagery, meditation, or other practices that enhance your ability to vividly imagine scenarios.

2. Involve Others: Collaborate with friends, family, or colleagues in this mental exercise. Discussing potential challenges and sharing strategies can provide diverse perspectives and additional insights.

3. Integrate with Goal Setting: Integrate this mental exercise with your goal-setting process. Envision challenges that may arise on the path to achieving your goals and plan responses accordingly. This alignment ensures that your strategies align with your broader objectives.

4. Combine with Positive Affirmations: Combine the mental exercise with positive affirmations. Affirmations can reinforce your belief in your ability to overcome challenges and contribute to a more positive and resilient mindset.

5. Adapt Frequency: Adjust the frequency of this exercise based on your needs and preferences. Some individuals may benefit from a more frequent practice, while others may find success with less frequent sessions.

By regularly engaging in this practical tool, individuals can develop a proactive mindset, enhance their preparedness for challenges, and cultivate resilience in the face of uncertainties. Envisioning potential obstacles and planning responses contribute to a more confident and adaptable approach to life's complexities.

38) Look for the Poetry in Ordinary Things:

Anecdote: Imagine a sunset. Beauty is often found in the simplest moments.

Interpretation: Cultivate gratitude by finding joy in everyday occurrences, embracing life's simple pleasures. Cultivate appreciation for the mundane aspects of life.

Practical Tool: Practice mindfulness, savoring ordinary moments with heightened awareness. Pause and find joy in everyday occurrences, fostering a sense of gratitude.

The practical tool involves practicing mindfulness by savoring ordinary moments with heightened awareness. This approach encourages individuals to pause, appreciate, and find joy in everyday occurrences, fostering a sense of gratitude.

Practicing Mindfulness:

1. Definition of Mindfulness: Mindfulness is the practice of being fully present and engaged in the current moment without judgment. It involves paying attention to one's thoughts, feelings, and surroundings with a sense of openness and acceptance.

2. Heightened Awareness: The tool emphasizes heightened awareness, encouraging individuals to engage their senses fully in the present moment. This includes noticing sights, sounds, smells, tastes, and tactile sensations with greater sensitivity.

Savoring Ordinary Moments:

1. Definition of Savoring: Savoring involves fully enjoying and appreciating positive experiences. It's about intentionally slowing down, acknowledging, and relishing the richness of a moment.

2. Ordinary Moments: The tool focuses on savoring ordinary moments, emphasizing that joy and fulfillment can be found in the simplicity of everyday life. It encourages individuals to recognize the beauty in mundane occurrences.

How to Implement the Tool:

1. Pause and Presence: Incorporate pauses into your daily routine. Whether it's during a morning walk, a meal, or a break at work, take a moment to pause and bring your attention to the present. Be fully present in the experience.

2. Engage Your Senses: Engage your senses consciously. Notice the details of your surroundings—the colors, textures, and sounds. Whether you're outdoors, indoors, or enjoying a meal, bring heightened awareness to what you see, hear, touch, taste, and smell.

3. Practice Gratitude: Cultivate gratitude by intentionally finding joy in ordinary moments. Express appreciation for the small pleasures, acknowledging the positive aspects of your current experience. This can be done mentally or by keeping a gratitude journal.

4. Mindful Breathing: Incorporate mindful breathing into your moments of pause. Focus on your breath, bringing your attention to the sensations of inhaling and exhaling. This simple practice helps anchor you in the present.

5. Limit Multitasking: Minimize multitasking during these moments of mindfulness. Instead, commit to fully engaging with one activity at a time. Whether it's enjoying a cup of tea, taking a walk, or listening to music, give it your undivided attention.

Benefits of Practicing Mindfulness and Savoring:

1. Increased Well-Being: Regular mindfulness practice has been associated with increased overall well-being. Savoring ordinary moments contributes to a positive emotional state and a greater sense of contentment.

2. Stress Reduction: Mindfulness is a proven tool for stress reduction. By focusing on the present and appreciating ordinary moments, individuals can alleviate stress and anxiety, fostering a more relaxed state of mind.

3. Enhanced Emotional Resilience: Practicing mindfulness and savoring builds emotional resilience. It helps individuals navigate challenges with greater composure and perspective, leading to a more balanced emotional well-being.

4. Improved Focus and Concentration: Mindfulness enhances cognitive abilities, including focus and concentration. By training the mind to be present, individuals can improve their attention span and perform tasks with greater efficiency.

5. Positive Outlook: Savoring ordinary moments promotes a positive outlook on life. It shifts the focus from what may be lacking to the abundance of small joys, fostering optimism and a deeper appreciation for the present.

Adapt to Your Preferences:

1. Mindful Activities: Integrate mindfulness into specific activities that resonate with you. Whether it's gardening, cooking, or reading, choose activities that bring you joy and lend themselves well to mindfulness.

2. Mindfulness Apps and Resources: Explore mindfulness apps and resources that offer guided meditations, mindful exercises, and prompts for savoring the present. These tools can provide additional support and structure to your practice.

3. Mindful Walking or Nature Observation: Incorporate mindful walking or nature observation into your routine. Take a leisurely stroll, paying attention to the sensations of each step or the beauty of the natural environment around you.

4. Mindful Eating: Practice mindful eating by savoring each bite of your meals. Pay attention to the flavors, textures, and aromas of the food. This can transform a routine meal into a mindful and enjoyable experience.

5. Share Moments of Mindfulness: Share moments of mindfulness with others. Whether it's enjoying a sunset, sharing a meal, or simply being present together, communal mindfulness can strengthen connections and deepen shared experiences.

By incorporating this practical tool into daily life, individuals can experience the transformative effects of mindfulness and savoring. The intentional focus on ordinary moments with heightened awareness fosters a sense of gratitude, contributing to overall well-being and a more fulfilling life.

39) To Do Wrong to One Is to Do Wrong to Yourself (Sympatheia):

Anecdote: Picture a network of interconnected threads. Harm to one affects the whole.

Interpretation: Recognize the shared humanity, fostering compassion and empathy. Recognize the interconnectedness of humanity; harming others harms yourself.

Practical Tool: Before acting, consider the impact on others, fostering a sense of shared well-being. Act with kindness and consideration, understanding the ripple effect of your actions. The practical tool involves considering the impact on others before acting, with the aim of fostering a sense of shared well-being. This approach encourages individuals to act with kindness and consideration, recognizing the ripple effect of their actions on the people around them.

Considering Impact on Others:

1. Empathy and Perspective-Taking: Before taking any action, cultivate empathy by considering the perspectives and feelings of others. Try to understand how your actions might be perceived and how they could impact the well-being of those involved.

2. Anticipating Consequences: Anticipate the potential consequences of your actions. Consider not only the immediate impact but also the longer-term effects on relationships, emotions, and the overall atmosphere within a given context.

Fostering a Sense of Shared Well-Being:

1. Shared Responsibility: Embrace the idea of shared responsibility for the well-being of those around you. Recognize that individual actions contribute to the collective experience, and by acting with consideration, you can positively influence the shared environment.

2. Kindness and Consideration: Prioritize kindness and consideration in your interactions. Act in ways that reflect respect, understanding, and a genuine concern for the feelings and needs of others. This can create a positive and supportive atmosphere.

3. Building Positive Relationships: Acknowledge that actions have the power to shape and strengthen relationships. Fostering a sense of shared well-being involves building and maintaining positive connections with others based on trust, compassion, and mutual support.

4. Collaboration and Cooperation: Actively seek opportunities for collaboration and cooperation. By considering the impact on others, you contribute to a culture of teamwork and shared goals, enhancing the overall well-being of the group or community.

How to Implement the Tool:

1. Reflect Before Acting: Take a moment to reflect before taking action. Consider the potential consequences and how your actions might affect the individuals involved. This reflective pause allows for a more intentional and thoughtful approach.

2. Put Yourself in Others' Shoes: Practice putting yourself in the shoes of others. Consider how you would feel if you were on the receiving end of the action you're about to take. This perspective-taking helps build empathy and guides considerate behavior.

3. Seek Feedback: If possible, seek feedback from others before making decisions that may impact them. Open communication and a willingness to understand different viewpoints contribute to a more collaborative and inclusive approach.

4. Encourage Open Dialogue: Foster open dialogue within your interactions. Encourage others to share their thoughts and feelings, creating a space where everyone's perspectives are valued. This openness contributes to a sense of shared well-being.

5. Express Gratitude: Express gratitude and appreciation for the contributions of others. Acknowledge their efforts and positive impact, reinforcing a culture of recognition and shared well-being.

Benefits of Considering Impact on Others:

1. Positive Work Environment: Considering the impact on others contributes to a positive work or social environment. When individuals act with kindness and consideration, it fosters a culture of collaboration, support, and mutual respect.

2. Enhanced Relationships: Thoughtful actions strengthen relationships. By taking into account how your actions affect others, you build trust and create a foundation for positive and lasting connections.

3. Conflict Prevention: Proactively considering the impact on others can help prevent conflicts. It allows individuals to navigate potential challenges with sensitivity, reducing the likelihood of misunderstandings or tensions.

4. Improved Communication: Open and considerate communication is a natural outcome of this tool. By thinking about the impact on others, individuals are more likely to communicate effectively and with empathy, fostering understanding.

5. Increased Collective Well-Being: The ripple effect of actions that prioritize shared well-being contributes to an increased sense of collective well-being. Individuals feel valued, supported, and part of a community that cares about their experiences and contributions.

Adapt to Your Preferences:

1. Cultural Sensitivity: Adapt your approach to consider cultural differences and individual preferences. What may be perceived as considerate in one cultural context may differ in another. Respect diverse perspectives and adjust your actions accordingly.

2. Flexibility in Decision-Making: Be flexible in your decision-making process. Recognize that situations may evolve, and adjustments may be needed to ensure continued consideration for the well-being of others.

3. Encourage Feedback Loops: Establish feedback loops within your personal or professional relationships. Encourage others to provide feedback on how your actions impact them, fostering continuous improvement and a shared commitment to well-being.

4. Collaborative Decision-Making: Embrace collaborative decision-making processes. Involve others in the decision-making where appropriate, ensuring that diverse perspectives are considered and contributing to a sense of shared responsibility.
5. Educate and Promote Awareness: Promote awareness and education within your community or workplace about the importance of considering the impact on others. Encourage a culture that values empathetic actions and prioritizes shared well-being.

By incorporating this practical tool into daily interactions, individuals can contribute to a positive and supportive environment. Considering the impact on others before acting fosters a culture of kindness, collaboration, and shared well-being, ultimately enhancing relationships and the overall quality of interpersonal experiences.

40) Always Choose "Alive Time":

Anecdote: Imagine two clocks—one ticking, one stagnant. Engage in activities that make you feel alive.

Interpretation: Opt for activities that enrich life, avoiding passive pursuits that contribute to stagnation. Opt for experiences that bring fulfillment and vitality

Practical Tool: Prioritize activities that align with your goals, passions, and contribute to personal growth.

The practical tool involves prioritizing activities that align with your goals, passions, and contribute to personal growth. This approach emphasizes intentional decision-making in how time and energy are allocated, with a focus on activities that align with one's broader objectives.

Prioritizing Activities:

1. Alignment with Goals: Consider your short-term and long-term goals. Prioritize activities that directly contribute to the achievement of these goals. This ensures that your time and efforts are directed toward outcomes that matter to you.

2. Passion Alignment: Identify your passions and interests. Prioritize activities that align with these passions, as engaging in what you love can bring fulfillment, motivation, and a sense of purpose to your life.

3. Contributing to Personal Growth: Evaluate activities based on their potential to contribute to your personal growth. Prioritize experiences that challenge you, provide opportunities for learning, and support your development in various aspects of life.

How to Implement the Tool:

1. Define Your Goals: Clearly define your goals, both short-term and long-term. This could include career objectives, personal development goals, or aspirations in various areas of life. Having a clear vision informs your activity prioritization.

2. Identify Your Passions: Reflect on your passions and interests. What activities energize you and bring you joy? Identify the areas of your life where you feel most fulfilled, and use this awareness to guide your prioritization.

3. Create a Priority List: Develop a priority list that aligns with your goals and passions. This list serves as a guide for decision-

making, helping you allocate time and resources to activities that matter most to you.

4. Time Management: Practice effective time management. Allocate time to high-priority activities first, ensuring that essential and growth-oriented tasks are given precedence in your schedule.

5. Regular Evaluation: Regularly evaluate your activities and commitments. Assess whether they still align with your goals and passions. Adjust your priorities as needed, allowing for flexibility as your goals and interests evolve.

Benefits of Prioritizing Activities:

1. Goal Achievement: Prioritizing activities aligned with your goals increases the likelihood of goal achievement. It directs your efforts toward actions that move you closer to the outcomes you desire.

2. Enhanced Focus: Focusing on high-priority activities enhances your overall focus. It reduces distractions and ensures that your energy is concentrated on tasks that contribute meaningfully to your objectives.

3. Increased Satisfaction: Engaging in activities that align with your passions brings a sense of satisfaction and fulfillment. When you prioritize what you love, you're more likely to find joy and purpose in your daily pursuits.

4. Continuous Learning: Prioritizing activities that contribute to personal growth fosters a mindset of continuous learning. It encourages you to seek out challenges, acquire new skills, and evolve in both personal and professional capacities.

5. Efficient Resource Utilization: Efficiently allocate your resources, including time and energy. Prioritizing activities ensures that these resources are invested in endeavors that yield the most significant returns in terms of personal and professional development.

Adapt to Your Preferences:

1. Seasonal Priorities: Recognize that priorities may shift based on seasons of life or changing circumstances. Adapt your priorities to align with your current context, allowing for flexibility as your goals and passions evolve.
2. Balance Multiple Interests: If you have multiple passions, find a balance that allows you to engage in a variety of activities. Prioritize based on your current focus while still allocating time for other interests over time.
3. Delegate or Decline: Learn to delegate tasks that don't align with your core goals or passions. If possible, say no to commitments that do not contribute to your personal or professional growth. This allows you to focus on what truly matters.
4. Mindful Decision-Making: Practice mindful decision-making. Before committing to an activity, assess whether it aligns with your priorities. Consider the impact on your goals and passions, ensuring that your decisions are intentional.
5. Periodic Reflection: Periodically reflect on your priorities and revisit your goals. This reflection allows you to assess your progress, make adjustments as needed, and ensure that your activities align with your evolving aspirations.

By implementing this practical tool, individuals can create a purpose-driven and fulfilling life. Prioritizing activities based on alignment with goals, passions, and personal growth ensures that time and energy are invested in pursuits that contribute meaningfully to one's overall well-being and success.

41) Associate Only with People That Make You Better:

Anecdote: Picture a team rowing towards a common goal. Surrounding yourself with positive influences propels you forward.

Interpretation: Choose relationships that uplift and challenge, contributing positively to your character. Your environment shapes you; choose relationships that foster growth.

Practical Tool: Evaluate relationships regularly, ensuring they align with your values and contribute to growth. Evaluate relationships regularly, nurturing those that contribute positively to your well-being.

The practical tool involves regularly evaluating relationships to ensure they align with your values and contribute to personal growth. The emphasis is on nurturing relationships that positively impact your well-being.

Regular Relationship Evaluation:

1. Assess Alignment with Values: Regularly assess whether your relationships align with your core values. Consider the values that are important to you, such as integrity, trust, respect, and empathy. Evaluate whether the dynamics within your relationships reflect these values.

2. Reflect on Personal Growth: Reflect on how each relationship contributes to your personal growth. Consider whether the people in your life support your aspirations, encourage your development, and provide constructive feedback. Evaluate whether the relationships foster a positive and nurturing environment for growth.

Nurturing Positive Relationships:

1. Open Communication: Foster open communication within your relationships. Create a space where honest and transparent conversations can take place. This allows you to express your needs, expectations, and concerns, contributing to a deeper understanding between individuals.

2. Mutual Support: Cultivate relationships where there is mutual support. Assess whether the people in your life encourage and uplift you during both challenging and joyful times. Likewise, strive to be a source of support for others.

3. Shared Values and Goals: Prioritize relationships with individuals who share similar values and goals. When there is alignment in fundamental beliefs and aspirations, it strengthens the foundation of the relationship and contributes to a sense of shared purpose.

4. Boundary Setting: Establish and maintain healthy boundaries within your relationships. Evaluate whether there is mutual respect for personal space, opinions, and boundaries. Healthy boundaries contribute to a balanced and respectful dynamic.

5. Quality Time: Invest quality time in relationships that matter most to you. Regularly engaging in meaningful interactions

strengthens connections and reinforces the importance of the relationship in your life.

How to Implement the Tool:

1. Regular Check-Ins: Schedule regular check-ins with yourself to evaluate the state of your relationships. This could be a monthly or quarterly practice where you reflect on the dynamics, communication, and overall satisfaction within each relationship.

2. Journaling: Use journaling as a tool for reflection. Write about your experiences, emotions, and observations within your relationships. Journaling provides a tangible record that can aid in the evaluation process.

3. Feedback and Communication: Seek feedback from trusted friends, family, or mentors. Honest feedback can provide valuable insights into the health of your relationships and areas for improvement. Foster open communication channels to discuss relationship dynamics.

4. Mindful Observation: Practice mindful observation of your feelings and experiences within each relationship. Pay attention to how you feel when interacting with others and whether those feelings align with positive or negative aspects of the relationship.

5. Set Relationship Goals: Establish goals for your relationships. These goals could be centered around improving communication, deepening emotional connection, or supporting each other's growth. Regularly assess progress toward these goals.

Benefits of Relationship Evaluation:

1. Increased Well-Being: Regularly evaluating relationships contributes to increased overall well-being. By nurturing positive connections and addressing challenges, individuals can create a supportive and fulfilling social network.

2. Healthy Boundaries: Relationship evaluation reinforces the importance of healthy boundaries. Recognizing and setting boundaries helps maintain respectful interactions and prevents potential sources of stress or conflict.

3. Personal Growth and Development: Relationships that contribute to personal growth enhance an individual's development. By surrounding yourself with supportive and encouraging individuals, you are more likely to overcome challenges and achieve your goals.

4. Improved Communication: Open and honest communication is a natural outcome of relationship evaluation. Regular assessments encourage individuals to express their needs and concerns, fostering better understanding and communication.

5. Quality Connections: Prioritizing relationships that align with your values results in quality connections. These connections go beyond surface-level interactions, creating meaningful relationships that bring joy, support, and fulfillment.

Adapt to Your Preferences:

1. Frequency of Evaluation: Adjust the frequency of relationship evaluation based on your preferences. Some individuals may

prefer more frequent check-ins, while others may find quarterly or yearly assessments more suitable.

2. Customized Evaluation Criteria: Customize the criteria for evaluating relationships based on your unique values and priorities. What matters most to you in a relationship? Tailor your assessment to align with your personal preferences.

3. Relationship Building Activities: Integrate relationship-building activities into your routine. Engage in shared hobbies, experiences, or conversations that strengthen connections and contribute positively to the dynamics of the relationship.

4. Professional Relationships: Extend the evaluation tool to professional relationships. Assess how your professional connections align with your career goals and contribute to your professional development.

5. Mindful Disconnection: Acknowledge that some relationships may not align with your values or contribute positively to your well-being. Practice mindful disconnection when necessary, recognizing that letting go of certain relationships can be a healthy and necessary step for personal growth.

By implementing this practical tool, individuals can cultivate meaningful relationships that align with their values, contribute to personal growth, and enhance overall well-being. Regular evaluation ensures that relationships remain supportive, fulfilling, and aligned with one's aspirations and values.

42) If Someone Offends You, Realize You Are Complicit in Taking Offense:

Anecdote: Imagine a dialogue. Offense is a joint creation; choose not to participate.

Interpretation: Embrace the power to choose responses, avoiding unnecessary suffering from perceived offenses. Offense is often a choice; you have control over your reactions.

Practical Tool: When offended, pause to assess if taking offense is a conscious choice. Choose serenity. Reflect on why you feel offended and consider choosing a response of understanding or indifference. The practical tool involves a mindful approach to handling offense. It encourages individuals, when offended, to pause and assess whether taking offense is a conscious choice. The tool suggests choosing serenity and taking a reflective stance on why the offense was felt, considering responses of understanding or indifference.

Mindful Handling of Offense:

1. Pause and Assess: When faced with a situation that might cause offense, intentionally pause before reacting. This momentary pause allows you to assess your emotions and consider whether taking offense is a conscious choice or a reflexive reaction.

2. Conscious Choice of Serenity: Instead of automatically reacting with offense, make a conscious choice to prioritize serenity. This involves maintaining a calm and composed state of mind, even in the face of perceived slights or challenges.

Reflective Stance:

1. Understand the Source of Offense: Reflect on why you feel offended. Consider the specific words, actions, or circumstances that triggered the offense. Understanding the source of offense provides insight into your emotional reactions.

2. Consider Responses: Instead of reacting impulsively, consider alternative responses. Reflect on whether responding with understanding or indifference is a more constructive and mindful approach. This step involves choosing a response that aligns with your values and promotes a positive outcome.

How to Implement the Tool:

1. Develop Self-Awareness: Cultivate self-awareness to recognize when you are feeling offended. Develop an awareness of your emotional reactions and triggers. This heightened self-awareness is the first step in implementing the tool effectively.

2. Practice Mindful Breathing: Use mindful breathing as a tool to center yourself during moments of offense. Take a few deep breaths to create a sense of calmness and prevent impulsive reactions. Mindful breathing provides a valuable space for thoughtful reflection.

3. Reflect on Intentions: Reflect on your intentions when choosing to take offense. Ask yourself whether feeling offended serves a purpose or if it is a reaction based on habit. Consider whether choosing serenity aligns better with your overall well-being.

4. Evaluate the Significance: Evaluate the significance of the offense. Consider whether the situation warrants a strong

emotional reaction or if it can be viewed with a more detached perspective. This evaluation helps in determining the appropriate level of response.

5. Consider the Other Person's Perspective: Practice empathy by considering the other person's perspective. Reflect on their intentions, experiences, and potential misunderstandings. This perspective-taking can lead to a more understanding and empathetic response.

Benefits of Mindful Handling of Offense:

1. Emotional Resilience: Mindful handling of offense contributes to emotional resilience. Choosing serenity and responding thoughtfully instead of reactively builds emotional strength and adaptability.

2. Improved Communication: By taking a reflective stance, individuals can improve communication. Thoughtful responses foster better understanding and prevent escalation of conflicts that may arise from impulsive reactions.

3. Personal Growth: The tool promotes personal growth by encouraging individuals to reflect on their emotional responses. Understanding the sources of offense and choosing constructive responses contribute to continuous self-improvement.

4. Cultivation of Serenity: Choosing serenity as a conscious response contributes to a more peaceful state of mind. This approach enables individuals to navigate challenges with a calm demeanor, promoting overall well-being.

5. Enhanced Relationships: Mindful handling of offense contributes to healthier relationships. Choosing understanding or

indifference over reactive offense fosters a positive and constructive dynamic with others.

Adapt to Your Preferences:

1. Customize Response Strategies: Adapt response strategies based on the specific situation and your personal preferences. Consider alternative responses that align with your values and the context of the offense.

2. Seek Support and Guidance: Seek support from trusted friends, mentors, or counselors when faced with challenging situations. Discussing your feelings and seeking guidance can provide valuable perspectives and coping strategies.

3. Mindfulness Practices: Explore additional mindfulness practices that resonate with you. This could include meditation, mindfulness exercises, or mindfulness-based stress reduction techniques. Incorporate practices that enhance your ability to choose serenity.

4. Learn from Experiences: Learn from past experiences where you may have reacted impulsively to offense. Use these experiences as opportunities for growth and self-reflection. Identify patterns and develop strategies for more mindful responses in the future.

5. Educate Others on Mindful Communication: Encourage mindful communication within your social circles. Share the benefits of choosing serenity and responding thoughtfully to offenses. Promoting a culture of understanding and empathy contributes to a more harmonious environment.

By implementing this practical tool, individuals can navigate moments of offense with a mindful and intentional approach.

Choosing serenity and adopting a reflective stance contribute to emotional resilience, improved communication, and overall personal growth.

43) Fate Behaves as She Pleases...Do Not Forget This:

Anecdote: Picture a river's unpredictable flow. Life's twists are beyond control; adapt and navigate.

Interpretation: Embrace uncertainty. Stoicism teaches resilience in the face of life's unpredictable nature. Embrace the uncertainty of life, understanding that some events are beyond your influence.

Practical Tool: When plans go awry, reflect on the impermanence of circumstances, adapting with grace. Develop resilience by accepting the unpredictable nature of fate.

The practical tool involves responding to unexpected challenges or changes in plans with grace and resilience. It encourages individuals to reflect on the impermanence of circumstances and to adapt with acceptance.

Adapting with Grace and Resilience:

1. Reflection on Impermanence: When faced with unexpected changes or disruptions to plans, take a moment to reflect on the impermanence of circumstances. Understand that life is dynamic, and situations can change rapidly. This reflection serves as a reminder to approach challenges with a sense of impermanence.

2. Adaptation with Acceptance: Cultivate resilience by adapting to changes with acceptance. Rather than resisting or becoming frustrated, choose to navigate the situation with a mindset of

acceptance. This involves acknowledging the unpredictability of life and being open to new possibilities.

How to Implement the Tool:

1. Mindful Reflection: Engage in mindful reflection when plans deviate from the expected course. Take a step back and recognize that circumstances are transient. This awareness helps in reframing the situation and approaching it with a calm and composed mindset.

2. Practice Acceptance: Practice the art of acceptance. Instead of dwelling on what went wrong or what didn't go as planned, focus on accepting the current reality. Acknowledge that unexpected changes are a natural part of life, and by embracing them, you can reduce stress and anxiety.

3. Flexibility in Thinking: Cultivate flexibility in your thinking. Be open to alternative solutions and outcomes. A flexible mindset allows you to adapt more easily to unexpected changes and find creative solutions to challenges.

4. Learn from the Experience: View unexpected changes as opportunities for learning and growth. Consider what lessons can be derived from the situation. This proactive approach transforms challenges into valuable experiences that contribute to personal development.

5. Resilience Building: Use each instance of adapting to changes as an opportunity to build resilience. Resilience involves bouncing back from setbacks and facing adversity with strength. By developing a resilient mindset, you become better equipped to handle future uncertainties.

Benefits of Adapting with Grace:

1. Reduced Stress: Responding to unexpected changes with grace reduces stress. Acceptance and adaptability allow individuals to navigate challenges without becoming overwhelmed by negative emotions.

2. Improved Mental Well-Being: Embracing the impermanence of circumstances contributes to improved mental well-being. A mindset of acceptance fosters peace of mind and emotional stability in the face of uncertainties.

3. Enhanced Problem-Solving Skills: Responding gracefully to unexpected changes enhances problem-solving skills. Individuals who can adapt to new circumstances with composure are better equipped to find effective and creative solutions.

4. Positive Relationships: Adapting with grace contributes to positive relationships. When individuals can navigate changes without undue stress, it positively influences their interactions with others, creating a harmonious social environment.

5. Personal Growth: Embracing the unpredictability of life fosters personal growth. Each challenge and unexpected change becomes an opportunity for learning, resilience building, and self-improvement.

Adapt to Your Preferences:

1. Mindfulness Practices: Incorporate mindfulness practices into your routine. Mindfulness can help you stay present in the moment and approach challenges with a calm and focused mindset.

2. Journaling: Maintain a journal to document your reflections on unexpected changes. Journaling provides a space for processing emotions, gaining insights, and tracking personal growth over time.
3. Community Support: Seek support from your community or social circles. Sharing experiences with others can provide valuable perspectives and emotional support, enhancing your ability to adapt with grace.
4. Celebrate Adaptability: Celebrate your adaptability and resilience. Acknowledge and reward yourself for handling unexpected changes with grace. This positive reinforcement reinforces the value of a flexible and accepting mindset.
5. Continuous Learning: Embrace a mindset of continuous learning. Recognize that each experience, whether planned or unexpected, offers opportunities for growth and development. Approach life as an ongoing journey of learning and adaptation.

By implementing this practical tool, individuals can cultivate a mindset of acceptance and resilience in the face of unexpected changes. Reflecting on the impermanence of circumstances and adapting with grace contributes to reduced stress, improved mental well-being, and a positive approach to life's uncertainties.

44) Possessions Are Yours Only in Trust:

Anecdote: Imagine holding a fragile gift. Possessions are temporary; treat them with care.

Interpretation: Possessions are temporary. Stoicism teaches detachment, valuing experiences over material wealth. Material wealth is transient; prioritize relationships and experiences.

Practical Tool: Reflect on the impermanence of material possessions, focusing on their utility rather than attachment. Cultivate a mindset of stewardship, using possessions responsibly and appreciating their impermanence.

The practical tool encourages individuals to reflect on the impermanence of material possessions, emphasizing utility over attachment. It promotes a mindset of stewardship, where possessions are used responsibly, and their impermanence is appreciated.

Mindful Reflection on Possessions:

1. Contemplation of Impermanence: Begin by reflecting on the impermanence of material possessions. Understand that everything in the material world is subject to change and eventual decay. This contemplation serves as a foundation for adopting a more mindful and responsible approach to possessions.

2. Utility Focus over Attachment: Shift the focus from attachment to utility. Instead of forming strong emotional attachments to material possessions, consider their practical value and usefulness in your life. This shift in perspective helps in reducing dependency on possessions for emotional fulfillment.

Cultivating a Stewardship Mindset:

1. Responsible Use: Cultivate a sense of responsibility in the use of possessions. Understand that as a steward, you are entrusted with the care and responsible use of the items you own. This mindset encourages conscious consumption and reduces unnecessary accumulation.

2. Appreciation of Impermanence: Appreciate the impermanence of possessions as a natural part of their life cycle. Recognize that items may serve their purpose for a specific period, and their value lies in their utility rather than in their permanence. This appreciation minimizes the emotional impact of letting go.

How to Implement the Tool:

1. Regular Reflection Practice: Set aside time for regular reflection on your possessions. This could be a monthly or quarterly practice where you assess the utility of each item and reflect on whether it aligns with your current needs and lifestyle.

2. Mindful Consumption: Practice mindful consumption when acquiring new possessions. Before making a purchase, consider the actual utility and necessity of the item. Mindful consumption reduces impulsive buying and ensures that possessions serve a meaningful purpose in your life.

3. Decluttering Rituals: Engage in decluttering rituals periodically. Assess your possessions and identify items that are no longer serving a purpose. Embrace the act of letting go, acknowledging that it creates space for new experiences and prevents unnecessary accumulation.

4. Quality over Quantity: Prioritize quality over quantity when acquiring possessions. Invest in items that are well-made, durable, and have long-lasting utility. Quality possessions often provide more value in the long run and are less likely to contribute to a disposable culture.

5. Mindful Maintenance: Practice mindful maintenance of your possessions. Regularly assess the condition of items and address any repairs or maintenance needs promptly. This approach extends the lifespan of possessions and fosters a sense of care and responsibility.

Benefits of Reflecting on Possessions:

1. Reduced Materialism: Reflecting on the impermanence of possessions reduces materialistic tendencies. Individuals become less focused on accumulating possessions for the sake of ownership and more mindful of the value each item brings to their lives.

2. Emotional Detachment: Embracing a utility-focused mindset promotes emotional detachment from possessions. This detachment allows individuals to let go of items more easily when needed, reducing the emotional burden associated with ownership.

3. Sustainable Living: The tool contributes to sustainable living practices. By appreciating the impermanence of possessions and adopting responsible stewardship, individuals contribute to a more sustainable and environmentally conscious lifestyle.

4. Financial Consciousness: Reflecting on possessions encourages financial consciousness. Individuals are more likely to make

intentional and considered purchasing decisions, avoiding unnecessary expenses and focusing on items that truly enhance their lives.

5. Enhanced Gratitude: The practice fosters a sense of gratitude for the possessions individuals have. By appreciating the utility and impermanence of items, individuals develop a deeper appreciation for the value each possession brings to their lives.

Adapt to Your Preferences:

1. Minimalism Practices: Explore minimalism practices as a complement to this tool. Minimalism emphasizes intentional living with a focus on essentials, aligning well with the utility-focused and impermanence-aware mindset.

2. Mindful Gift-Giving: Extend the reflection to gift-giving practices. When offering or receiving gifts, consider the utility and long-term value of the item rather than focusing solely on the act of giving or receiving.

3. Digital Possessions Reflection: Extend the reflection to digital possessions, such as files, photos, and online subscriptions. Regularly assess the digital clutter and ensure that digital possessions align with your current needs and priorities.

4. Educate Others: Share the benefits of reflecting on possessions with friends and family. Encourage responsible stewardship and mindful consumption within your social circles, fostering a community that values the utility and impermanence of material items.

5. Mindful Donations: Consider mindful donations as part of the reflection process. Items that are no longer serving a purpose for

you may be valuable to others. Donating possessions can be a meaningful way to extend the lifecycle of items while contributing to the well-being of others.

By implementing this practical tool, individuals can foster a healthier relationship with material possessions, focusing on their utility, embracing impermanence, and adopting a stewardship mindset. This approach leads to reduced materialism, enhanced emotional well-being, and a more sustainable lifestyle.

45) Don't Make Your Problems Worse by Bemoaning Them:

Anecdote: Picture a leaky boat. Complaining about the water won't fix the leak; take action instead.

Interpretation: Bemoaning magnifies problems. Stoicism advocates constructive action over self-pity. Complaining prolongs problems; focus on solutions.

Practical Tool: When facing challenges, focus on solutions and actionable steps instead of dwelling on difficulties. Channel energy into problem-solving rather than dwelling on difficulties.

The practical tool encourages individuals to adopt a solution-oriented mindset when faced with challenges. It emphasizes the importance of focusing on actionable steps and problem-solving rather than dwelling on difficulties.

Solution-Oriented Mindset:

1. Immediate Shift of Focus: When challenges arise, make an immediate shift in focus from the difficulties themselves to potential solutions. This mental shift is crucial for redirecting energy toward constructive problem-solving.

2. Problem-Solving Approach: Adopt a problem-solving approach that involves breaking down challenges into manageable components. Identify specific aspects of the problem that can be addressed, and concentrate on developing actionable steps to overcome each component.

How to Implement the Tool:

1. Assess the Challenge Objectively: Begin by objectively assessing the challenge at hand. Identify the key components, factors, or obstacles contributing to the difficulty. This step lays the foundation for a more structured and targeted problem-solving process.
2. Define Clear Objectives: Clearly define your objectives in addressing the challenge. What specific outcomes do you want to achieve? This clarity helps in creating a roadmap for problem-solving and ensures that efforts are directed toward meaningful goals.
3. Generate Actionable Steps: Break down the challenge into actionable steps. Focus on identifying specific tasks or actions that can be taken to address each aspect of the problem. This step transforms the challenge into a series of manageable tasks.
4. Prioritize Tasks: Prioritize the identified tasks based on their importance and impact. Determine which actions need to be addressed first to create a logical and effective sequence of steps. Prioritization ensures that efforts are directed toward the most critical aspects of the challenge.
5. Allocate Resources: Assess the resources available to you—whether they be time, skills, or external support. Allocate

resources strategically to support the implementation of your actionable steps. Efficient resource allocation enhances the likelihood of successful problem resolution.

Benefits of a Solution-Oriented Mindset:

1. Increased Productivity: Focusing on solutions and actionable steps leads to increased productivity. Rather than getting stuck in the challenges, individuals channel their energy into concrete actions that move them closer to resolution.

2. Positive Outlook: A solution-oriented mindset fosters a positive outlook. By concentrating on potential solutions, individuals maintain an optimistic perspective, which contributes to resilience and motivation during challenging times.

3. Efficient Problem Resolution: The tool facilitates more efficient problem resolution. By breaking down challenges into actionable steps, individuals address specific components of the problem systematically, leading to a more effective and timely resolution.

4. Empowerment: Adopting a solution-oriented mindset empowers individuals to take control of their circumstances. Rather than feeling overwhelmed by difficulties, they become active participants in the problem-solving process, experiencing a sense of agency.

5. Continuous Improvement: The tool supports a culture of continuous improvement. Individuals who consistently focus on solutions develop a mindset geared toward learning and adapting. Challenges become opportunities for growth and enhancement.

Adapt to Your Preferences:

1. Collaborative Problem-Solving: If appropriate, involve others in the problem-solving process. Collaborative efforts often bring diverse perspectives and ideas, enriching the solution-oriented approach. Collective problem-solving can also distribute the workload and resources more effectively.

2. Regular Review and Adjustment: Regularly review the progress of your solution-oriented efforts. If certain actions are not yielding the expected results, be open to adjusting your approach. Flexibility and adaptability are key to successful problem resolution.

3. Celebrate Achievements: Celebrate achievements along the way. Recognize and acknowledge the progress made, even if it's incremental. Celebrating achievements reinforces a positive mindset and provides motivation for continued efforts.

4. Reflect on Lessons Learned: Reflect on lessons learned during the problem-solving process. Each challenge presents an opportunity for learning and growth. Identifying lessons learned contributes to personal and professional development.

5. Integrate with Time Management: Integrate a solution-oriented approach with effective time management. Allocate dedicated time for problem-solving activities, ensuring that you can focus on generating solutions without unnecessary distractions.

By implementing this practical tool, individuals can cultivate a proactive and resilient mindset when facing challenges. Focusing on solutions and actionable steps promotes efficiency, positive outlook, and continuous improvement, ultimately contributing to effective problem resolution.

46) Accept Success Without Arrogance, Handle Failure with Indifference:

Anecdote: Imagine a scale. Balance success and failure with humility and resilience.

Interpretation: Stoicism encourages a balanced response to success and failure, avoiding extremes. Maintain a steady demeanor regardless of external outcomes.

Practical Tool: Cultivate humility in success and resilience in failure, acknowledging both as part of life's journey. Celebrate achievements without ego, and view failures as opportunities to learn and grow.

The practical tool encourages individuals to cultivate humility in success and resilience in failure, recognizing both as integral parts of life's journey. It emphasizes celebrating achievements without ego and viewing failures as opportunities for learning and growth.

Cultivating Humility and Resilience:

1. Acknowledge Success with Humility: When achieving success, practice acknowledging it with humility. Avoid excessive pride or ego, and recognize that success often involves a combination of personal efforts and external factors. Humility fosters gratitude, a sense of interconnectedness, and a balanced perspective on accomplishments.

2. Resilience in the Face of Failure: Embrace failure as a natural part of life's journey. Develop resilience by viewing failures not

as setbacks but as opportunities to learn, adapt, and grow. Resilience enables individuals to bounce back from challenges, maintaining a positive outlook despite setbacks.

How to Implement the Tool:

1. Mindful Reflection on Achievements: When experiencing success, engage in mindful reflection. Recognize the contributions of others, acknowledge the role of external factors, and express gratitude for the opportunities that led to success. This reflective practice helps in maintaining humility.

2. Learn from Failures: Approach failures with a learning mindset. Instead of dwelling on disappointment or frustration, analyze the factors that contributed to the failure. Identify lessons learned and consider how the experience can be leveraged for personal and professional growth.

3. Balanced Celebration of Success: Celebrate achievements in a balanced manner. While it's essential to acknowledge and celebrate success, do so without excessive pride or arrogance. Share credit with collaborators, express gratitude, and maintain a grounded perspective on accomplishments.

4. Cultivate a Growth Mindset: Cultivate a growth mindset that sees challenges and failures as opportunities for development. Embrace the belief that abilities and intelligence can be developed through dedication and hard work. A growth mindset fosters resilience and a positive approach to both success and failure.

5. Seek Feedback and Guidance: Actively seek feedback, especially during challenging times. Whether successful or facing failure,

constructive feedback provides valuable insights. Embrace feedback as a tool for continuous improvement and use it to inform future actions.

Benefits of Cultivating Humility and Resilience:

1. Enhanced Emotional Well-Being: Cultivating humility and resilience contributes to enhanced emotional well-being. Balancing success with humility and viewing failures constructively fosters emotional stability and a positive overall mindset.

2. Improved Relationships: Humility in success creates positive relationships by avoiding arrogance or a sense of superiority. Resilience in failure enables individuals to navigate setbacks without placing undue burden on relationships, fostering support and understanding.

3. Continuous Personal Growth: The tool supports continuous personal growth. By approaching success and failure as opportunities for learning, individuals consistently evolve and develop new skills. This growth mindset is fundamental to adapting to life's challenges.

4. Effective Leadership: Leaders who cultivate humility and resilience inspire trust and loyalty in their teams. They are approachable in success, fostering collaboration, and remain composed in the face of failure, providing guidance and support to their teams.

5. Adaptability in the Face of Challenges: Individuals who embrace both success and failure with humility and resilience become more adaptable in the face of challenges. They are better

equipped to navigate uncertainties and make informed decisions based on a balanced perspective.

Adapt to Your Preferences:

1. Practice Gratitude Rituals: Incorporate gratitude practices into your routine, especially during successful moments. Expressing gratitude fosters humility and a sense of appreciation for the contributions of others and external factors.

2. Mentorship and Peer Support: Seek mentorship and peer support during both successful and challenging times. Having mentors and a supportive network provides guidance and diverse perspectives, contributing to resilience and a balanced approach to achievements and setbacks.

3. Share Failure Stories: Share stories of failure openly with others. Creating a culture that normalizes discussing failures reduces stigma and encourages a collective approach to learning and growth. This openness fosters resilience within a community.

4. Mindful Practices: Integrate mindful practices, such as meditation or mindfulness exercises, into your routine. Mindfulness helps in maintaining a balanced perspective, reducing ego-driven reactions to success and providing clarity in navigating challenges.

5. Celebrate Others' Success: Actively celebrate the success of others without comparison or competition. Celebrating others' achievements contributes to a positive and supportive environment, reinforcing the importance of humility and collaborative growth.

By implementing this practical tool, individuals can navigate the complexities of success and failure with grace, humility, and resilience. Balancing achievements without ego and approaching failures as opportunities for learning fosters a mindset conducive to continuous personal growth and positive relationships.

47) Courage. Temperance. Justice. Wisdom. (Always):

Anecdote: Picture a compass. These virtues guide your moral and ethical decisions.

Interpretation: Practicing these virtues ensures a balanced and virtuous life, guiding actions and decisions. Uphold these virtues in all circumstances.

Practical Tool: Regularly assess actions against these virtues, striving for alignment in daily choices. Regularly reflect on your actions in light of these virtues, adjusting your behavior accordingly. The practical tool involves regularly assessing your actions against a set of virtues, striving for alignment in daily choices. It emphasizes the importance of reflection and adjustment based on these virtues.

Regular Assessment Against Virtues:

1. Define Your Virtues: Begin by clearly defining the virtues that hold significance for you. These virtues could include qualities such as honesty, integrity, kindness, compassion, resilience, humility, or any other values that align with your principles and beliefs.

2. Create a Virtue Framework: Establish a framework that outlines the virtues you want to prioritize. This framework serves as a guide for assessing your actions and behavior. It provides a clear

reference point for understanding the qualities you aim to embody in your daily life.

How to Implement the Tool:

1. Reflect on Daily Actions: Regularly set aside time for reflection on your daily actions. Consider the choices you made, interactions you had, and decisions you implemented. Assess these against the virtues you've identified as important, examining whether your behavior aligns with these values.

2. Identify Alignment and Misalignment: Identify instances where your actions align with the chosen virtues, acknowledging these moments of virtue embodiment. Similarly, recognize situations where your behavior may have deviated from the virtues. This identification is crucial for understanding areas of improvement.

3. Adjust Behavior Accordingly: Based on your reflections, make a conscious effort to adjust your behavior when misalignments with the chosen virtues are identified. Consider alternative actions or responses that better reflect the virtues you value. This process of adjustment contributes to ongoing personal development.

4. Set Virtue-Based Intentions: Before engaging in specific activities or interactions, set intentions aligned with your chosen virtues. This proactive approach helps in shaping your behavior in a manner consistent with your values. It serves as a prelude to mindful decision-making.

5. Seek Feedback on Virtue Alignment: Solicit feedback from trusted friends, mentors, or family members regarding your alignment with chosen virtues. External perspectives can provide

valuable insights and help you gain a more comprehensive understanding of how your actions are perceived in relation to your values.

Benefits of Regular Virtue Assessment:

1. Enhanced Self-Awareness: Regularly assessing actions against virtues enhances self-awareness. Individuals become more attuned to their behavior and the values that guide them, fostering a deeper understanding of personal strengths and areas for improvement.

2. Consistent Values Alignment: The tool promotes consistent alignment with chosen values. By regularly assessing actions against virtues, individuals establish a pattern of behavior that is in harmony with their core values, creating a sense of integrity and authenticity.

3. Continuous Personal Growth: This practice contributes to continuous personal growth. The awareness gained through reflection and adjustment supports ongoing development, allowing individuals to refine their character and embody virtues more consistently over time.

4. Improved Decision-Making: Aligning actions with chosen virtues leads to improved decision-making. Individuals who prioritize virtues in their choices are more likely to make ethical and values-driven decisions, even in challenging situations.

5. Positive Impact on Relationships: Virtue-based actions positively impact relationships. Consistent alignment with virtues fosters trust, respect, and understanding in personal and professional

connections, contributing to healthier and more fulfilling relationships.

Adapt to Your Preferences:

1. Customize Your Virtue Framework: Tailor the virtue framework to align with your unique values and priorities. Customize the list of virtues to reflect the qualities that resonate most deeply with your personal philosophy and aspirations.

2. Set Periodic Virtue Goals: Set specific virtue-based goals for yourself periodically. These goals can serve as benchmarks for your progress in aligning actions with virtues. Regularly revisit and adjust these goals based on evolving priorities.

3. Incorporate Virtue Reflection into Routine: Integrate virtue reflection into your daily or weekly routine. Consistency in reflection enhances the effectiveness of the tool. Consider using journaling or mindfulness practices as part of your routine for virtue assessment.

4. Share Virtue Journeys with Others: Share your virtue assessment journey with others who may be interested or are working toward similar personal development goals. Creating a supportive community around virtue alignment can provide encouragement and accountability.

5. Celebrate Virtue Milestones: Celebrate milestones related to virtue alignment. Acknowledge and celebrate moments where your actions reflect the virtues you've prioritized. Positive reinforcement reinforces the importance of virtuous behavior in your life.

By implementing this practical tool, individuals can create a framework for virtue-based decision-making and cultivate a character aligned with their chosen values. Regular assessment and adjustment contribute to ongoing personal growth, self-awareness, and the development of meaningful and values-driven relationships.

48) The Obstacle Is the Way:

Anecdote: Visualize a hurdle on a track. Challenges are opportunities for growth and progress.

Interpretation: Adversity is a path to strength. Stoicism transforms obstacles into stepping stones. Face obstacles with resilience and a positive mindset.

Practical Tool: When facing challenges, reframe them as opportunities for learning and personal development. Reframe challenges as chances to develop skills and overcome limitations. The practical tool encourages individuals to reframe challenges as opportunities for learning and personal development. It emphasizes viewing difficulties not as setbacks but as chances to develop skills and overcome limitations.

Reframing Challenges for Learning and Development:

1. Shift in Perspective: When faced with challenges, intentionally shift your perspective. Instead of perceiving challenges as obstacles or setbacks, view them as opportunities for growth, learning, and personal development. This shift in mindset lays the foundation for a proactive approach to difficulties.

2. Identify Learning Objectives: Break down the challenge into specific learning objectives. What skills or knowledge can you

gain from overcoming this challenge? Identifying clear learning objectives provides direction and purpose in tackling the difficulty.

How to Implement the Tool:

1. Embrace a Growth Mindset: Cultivate a growth mindset that sees challenges as avenues for improvement. A growth mindset acknowledges that abilities and intelligence can be developed through dedication and learning. Embracing this mindset creates a positive foundation for reframing challenges.

2. Seek Learning Opportunities: Actively seek learning opportunities within each challenge. Consider how the situation can contribute to your personal and professional development. Identify specific skills, knowledge, or insights that can be gained through navigating the challenge.

3. Reflect on Previous Challenges: Reflect on past challenges you've overcome and the lessons learned. Recognize the personal development that resulted from overcoming obstacles. This retrospective perspective reinforces the idea that challenges are transformative experiences.

4. Set Development Goals: Set development goals related to the current challenge. Define what skills or qualities you want to enhance as a result of overcoming the difficulty. These goals provide a roadmap for personal growth and serve as motivation during challenging times.

5. Celebrate Small Wins: Acknowledge and celebrate small wins along the way. Recognize incremental progress and achievements, no matter how minor. Celebrating small wins

boosts morale and reinforces the positive connection between challenges and personal development.

Benefits of Reframing Challenges:

1. Resilience Building: Reframing challenges as opportunities for learning builds resilience. Individuals develop the ability to bounce back from setbacks and approach difficulties with a positive and proactive mindset.

2. Continuous Learning: The tool promotes a culture of continuous learning. By viewing challenges as learning opportunities, individuals adopt a mindset that values the acquisition of new skills and knowledge, contributing to ongoing personal and professional development.

3. Increased Adaptability: Reframing challenges fosters adaptability. Individuals become more flexible and open to change, recognizing that challenges are inherent in growth and can lead to improved adaptability in various aspects of life.

4. Positive Mindset: Embracing challenges as opportunities for learning fosters a positive mindset. This optimistic outlook contributes to improved mental well-being and allows individuals to approach difficulties with a sense of curiosity and enthusiasm.

5. Skill Development: Challenges become platforms for skill development. Whether it's problem-solving, resilience, communication, or other skills, individuals actively engage in honing and refining their abilities through overcoming challenges.

Adapt to Your Preferences:

1. Mentorship and Guidance: Seek mentorship or guidance from those who have faced similar challenges. Learning from others' experiences provides insights and strategies for personal development in the face of difficulties.

2. Collaborative Learning: Approach challenges collaboratively. Engage with others who may be experiencing similar challenges, fostering a collaborative learning environment. Shared experiences can lead to collective growth.

3. Document the Learning Journey: Document your learning journey during challenges. Keep a journal or record of the skills acquired, insights gained, and personal growth experienced as a result of overcoming difficulties. This documentation serves as a tangible reminder of your progress.

4. Incorporate Learning Rituals: Integrate learning rituals into your routine. Dedicate specific time for learning activities, whether it's reading, skill-building exercises, or reflective practices. Consistent learning rituals contribute to ongoing personal development.

5. Share Your Growth Story: Share your growth story with others. Whether through mentorship, public speaking, or written reflections, sharing how challenges have contributed to your personal development can inspire and motivate others to reframe their own difficulties.

By implementing this practical tool, individuals can transform challenges from sources of stress into opportunities for learning and personal development. Reframing difficulties as stepping stones to growth promotes resilience, a positive mindset, and a continuous journey of self-improvement.

49) Ego Is the Enemy:

Anecdote: Picture a balloon deflating. An inflated ego hinders personal and professional growth.

Interpretation: Stoicism warns against ego-driven actions, promoting humility and self-awareness. Ego blinds you to your flaws and inhibits learning.

Practical Tool: Regularly reflect on actions and decisions, ensuring they are not ego-driven but aligned with virtue. Practice humility, seeking feedback and acknowledging areas for improvement.

The practical tool encourages individuals to regularly reflect on their actions and decisions, ensuring that they are not ego-driven but aligned with virtue. It emphasizes the practice of humility, seeking feedback, and acknowledging areas for improvement.

Regular Reflection on Actions and Decisions:

1. Scheduled Reflection Time: Set aside dedicated time for regular reflection on your actions and decisions. This could be a daily practice, weekly check-in, or any frequency that suits your routine. Scheduled reflection allows for intentional self-assessment.

2. Create a Reflection Environment: Choose a quiet and contemplative environment for reflection. Minimize distractions to facilitate focused introspection. This environment helps create a conducive space for self-awareness and honest evaluation.

How to Implement the Tool:

1. Ego-Check: During reflection, consciously evaluate whether your actions and decisions were ego-driven. Consider whether personal pride, validation, or self-interest played a significant role. This ego-check is crucial for aligning behavior with virtue.

2. Virtue Alignment Assessment: Evaluate your actions and decisions in light of the virtues you value. Consider virtues such as honesty, integrity, kindness, humility, and others that resonate with your principles. Assess how well your behavior aligns with these virtues.

3. Seek External Feedback: Actively seek feedback from trusted individuals in your personal and professional circles. Others' perspectives can offer valuable insights into your behavior and decision-making. Be open to constructive criticism and diverse viewpoints.

4. Practice Humility: Cultivate humility in your reflections. Acknowledge that everyone is a work in progress and that there is always room for improvement. Embrace a humble attitude, recognizing that seeking growth is a continuous journey.

5. Acknowledge Areas for Improvement: Identify and acknowledge specific areas for improvement. Whether it's communication, empathy, or decision-making, pinpoint aspects of your behavior that could be enhanced. This acknowledgment sets the stage for intentional personal development.

Benefits of Regular Reflection and Humility:

1. Enhanced Self-Awareness: Regular reflection enhances self-awareness. Understanding the motivations behind your actions

and decisions contributes to a deeper sense of self-awareness, promoting conscious and virtue-aligned behavior.

2. Aligned Decision-Making: Practicing reflection ensures that your decision-making aligns with your values. By considering virtues during the decision-making process, you create a framework for making choices that resonate with your principles.

3. Strengthened Relationships: Humility in seeking feedback and acknowledging areas for improvement strengthens relationships. Others appreciate individuals who are open to growth and demonstrate a willingness to learn from their experiences.

4. Personal Growth Mindset: The tool fosters a personal growth mindset. Embracing humility and actively seeking areas for improvement contribute to a mindset that values continuous learning and development.

5. Authentic Leadership: Leaders who regularly reflect on their actions and decisions, practicing humility, are more likely to exhibit authentic leadership. This authenticity builds trust and credibility among team members, fostering a positive work environment.

Adapt to Your Preferences:

1. Utilize Reflective Tools: Explore reflective tools such as journals, self-assessment questionnaires, or guided reflection exercises. These tools can provide structure to your reflection process and prompt deeper insights.

2. Join Peer Reflection Groups: Form or join peer reflection groups where individuals share their experiences and insights. Peer

groups create a supportive environment for collective self-improvement and accountability.

3. Rotate Feedback Sources: Rotate the sources of feedback you seek. Consider feedback from peers, mentors, supervisors, and even friends. Diverse perspectives contribute to a more comprehensive understanding of your actions and decisions.

4. Set Improvement Goals: Based on your reflections, set specific improvement goals. These goals should be actionable and focused on enhancing areas identified during your reflection. Regularly revisit and adjust these goals as part of your growth journey.

5. Celebrate Virtue-Aligned Actions: Acknowledge and celebrate instances where your actions align with virtues. Positive reinforcement encourages the repetition of virtue-aligned behavior and reinforces your commitment to ethical decision-making.

By implementing this practical tool, individuals cultivate a habit of reflective practice that promotes virtue-aligned behavior and humility. Seeking feedback and acknowledging areas for improvement contribute to personal growth, enhanced self-awareness, and the development of authentic and virtuous leadership qualities.

50) Stillness Is the Key:

Anecdote: Imagine a calm lake. In stillness, clarity emerges.

Interpretation: Amidst life's turbulence, inner calm is a source of strength and clarity. Quiet the mind to make better decisions and find inner peace.

Practical Tool: Cultivate stillness through practices like meditation, providing a foundation for wise decision-making. Incorporate moments of stillness, whether through meditation or contemplative activities, to foster mental clarity.

The practical tool encourages individuals to cultivate stillness through practices like meditation, providing a foundation for wise decision-making. It emphasizes incorporating moments of stillness, whether through meditation or contemplative activities, to foster mental clarity.

Cultivating Stillness for Wise Decision-Making:

1. Understanding Stillness: Stillness involves a state of quietness and calm, both externally and internally. It is a mental and emotional state where the mind is free from excessive noise, allowing for clarity and focus. Cultivating stillness is about creating moments of peace amid the busyness of life.

2. Meditation as a Tool: Meditation is a powerful tool for cultivating stillness. It involves practices that encourage mindfulness, breath awareness, and present-moment focus. Meditation techniques vary, but the common thread is the intentional cultivation of inner calm and mental clarity.

How to Implement the Tool:

1. Schedule Moments of Stillness: Intentionally schedule moments of stillness in your daily routine. This could be a short meditation session in the morning, a mindful walk during lunch, or a quiet moment of reflection before bedtime. Regularity is key to reaping the benefits of stillness.

2. Explore Meditation Practices: Experiment with different meditation practices to find what resonates with you. This could include mindfulness meditation, loving-kindness meditation, body scan meditation, or transcendental meditation. Choose techniques that align with your preferences and goals.

3. Create a Dedicated Space: Establish a dedicated space for stillness practices. Whether it's a corner in your home, a quiet outdoor spot, or a specific room, having a designated space signals to your mind that it's time for introspection and tranquility.

4. Focus on Breath Awareness: Incorporate breath awareness into your stillness practices. Paying attention to your breath is a simple yet effective way to anchor your awareness in the present moment. This practice promotes relaxation and mental clarity.

5. Be Present in Daily Activities: Extend the concept of stillness to your daily activities. Practice being fully present and engaged in whatever you're doing, whether it's eating, walking, or working. Mindful presence in daily life contributes to an overall sense of calm and clarity.

Benefits of Cultivating Stillness:

1. Enhanced Mental Clarity: Stillness practices, especially meditation, enhance mental clarity. Clearing the mental clutter allows for better decision-making, as you can approach situations with a focused and calm mind.

2. Reduced Stress and Anxiety: Cultivating stillness reduces stress and anxiety. Regular moments of tranquility help regulate the nervous system, leading to a calmer overall state. This, in turn, positively impacts decision-making by reducing the influence of stress-related factors.

3. Improved Emotional Regulation: Stillness practices contribute to improved emotional regulation. When faced with decisions, having a stable emotional state allows for more rational and balanced choices, free from impulsive reactions.

4. Increased Self-Awareness: Stillness fosters increased self-awareness. Through introspective practices, individuals gain a deeper understanding of their thoughts, emotions, and motivations. This self-awareness is valuable in making decisions aligned with one's values.

5. Greater Resilience: Cultivating stillness builds greater resilience. When faced with challenges, individuals who regularly practice stillness are better equipped to navigate difficulties with composure and resilience, leading to wiser decision-making.

Adapt to Your Preferences:

1. Mindful Movement Practices: Explore mindful movement practices, such as yoga or tai chi, as alternatives to seated

meditation. These activities integrate physical movement with breath awareness, providing a dynamic way to cultivate stillness.

2. Nature Contemplation: Spend time in nature for contemplation. Whether it's a walk in the park, sitting by a river, or hiking in the mountains, nature offers a serene backdrop for stillness practices and mental clarity.

3. Technology Detox: Consider incorporating moments of stillness by detoxing from technology. Designate specific times during the day to disconnect from screens, creating an environment conducive to quiet reflection.

4. Silent Retreats: Participate in silent retreats for more extended periods of stillness. These retreats provide immersive experiences focused on introspection, meditation, and inner quietude.

5. Mindful Eating Practices: Transform daily activities like eating into mindful moments. Pay attention to the sensory experience of eating, savoring each bite, and allowing for a meditative approach to nourishing your body.

By implementing this practical tool, individuals can foster a foundation of stillness that contributes to mental clarity, emotional well-being, and wise decision-making. Whether through meditation, mindful activities, or contemplative practices, cultivating moments of calmness becomes a valuable asset in navigating the complexities of life with greater awareness and presence.

51) Don't Let the Past Control Your Present:

Anecdote: Picture a shadow lifting. Dwelling on the past casts shadows on the present.

Interpretation: Learn from the past but don't let it dictate your current choices.

Practical Tool: Acknowledge past experiences, extracting lessons without letting them overshadow your present.

The practical tool encourages individuals to acknowledge past experiences, extracting lessons without letting them overshadow the present. It emphasizes the importance of learning from the past while maintaining a focus on the present.

Acknowledging Past Experiences and Extracting Lessons:

1. Reflect on Past Experiences: Take intentional time to reflect on past experiences, both positive and challenging. This reflective process involves revisiting significant events, relationships, and decisions that have shaped your journey.

2. Extracting Lessons: Identify and extract valuable lessons from each past experience. Consider what worked well, what could have been done differently, and the insights gained. Extracting lessons involves discerning patterns, understanding cause and effect, and recognizing personal growth.

How to Implement the Tool:

1. Practice Mindful Reflection: Engage in mindful reflection rather than dwelling on the past. Mindful reflection involves observing thoughts and emotions without judgment. This practice allows

for a balanced exploration of past experiences without becoming overly attached to them.

2. Identify Patterns and Themes: Look for patterns and recurring themes across various experiences. Identify commonalities in your reactions, decision-making processes, and the outcomes of certain actions. Recognizing patterns provides deeper insights into your behavior.

3. Focus on Learning, Not Regret: Shift the focus from regret to learning. Instead of dwelling on mistakes or missed opportunities, concentrate on the lessons derived from those experiences. Viewing challenges as opportunities for growth reframes the narrative around past events.

4. Apply Lessons to the Present: Actively apply the lessons learned from past experiences to your present circumstances. Consider how insights gained can inform your decision-making, problem-solving, and interpersonal interactions in the current moment.

5. Release Unnecessary Baggage: Let go of unnecessary emotional baggage associated with past experiences. Acknowledge any lingering emotions, whether they be regret, guilt, or resentment, and consciously release them. This allows for a more liberated and present-focused mindset.

Benefits of Acknowledging Past Experiences:

1. Informed Decision-Making: Lessons from past experiences inform decision-making. Understanding what has worked well or presented challenges in the past provides a foundation for making more informed and strategic choices in the present.

2. Personal Growth and Development: Acknowledging past experiences contributes to personal growth. Extracted lessons pave the way for continuous development, enabling individuals to evolve and adapt based on their evolving understanding of themselves and their environments.
3. Improved Problem-Solving: Learning from past problem-solving approaches enhances your ability to tackle current challenges. Past experiences serve as a repository of strategies and insights that can be applied to navigate complex situations more effectively.
4. Enhanced Emotional Intelligence: Acknowledging past experiences contributes to emotional intelligence. Understanding your own emotional responses and recognizing patterns in how you handle emotions allows for greater self-awareness and emotional regulation.
5. Resilience Building: Past experiences, particularly challenging ones, build resilience. Acknowledging the lessons learned from overcoming obstacles strengthens your capacity to navigate future challenges with resilience and adaptability.

Adapt to Your Preferences:

1. Create a Lessons Journal: Maintain a lessons journal where you document key takeaways from various experiences. This journal serves as a reference point for insights gained and can be revisited during moments of reflection.
2. Seek External Perspectives: Seek feedback from trusted friends, mentors, or advisors. External perspectives can offer additional

insights into your past experiences and provide a more comprehensive understanding of the lessons learned.

3. Set Intentional Goals: Use the lessons extracted to set intentional goals for personal and professional growth. Align your aspirations with the insights gained from past experiences, creating a roadmap for future endeavors.

4. Practice Gratitude: Cultivate a sense of gratitude for the lessons learned, even in challenging experiences. Gratitude shifts the focus from dwelling on negativity to appreciating the growth opportunities embedded in each situation.

5. Integrate Reflection into Routine: Make reflection on past experiences a regular part of your routine. Whether through daily journaling or weekly reflections, incorporating this practice into your life ensures a consistent and ongoing process of learning and growth.

By implementing this practical tool, individuals can strike a balance between honoring the lessons of the past and embracing the present. Acknowledging past experiences without being weighed down by them fosters a mindset of continuous learning, adaptability, and resilience.

52) Understand the Power of Your Thoughts:

Anecdote: Imagine a garden. Your mind is the soil; thoughts are the seeds.

Interpretation: Your thoughts shape your reality; cultivate a positive mental landscape.

Practical Tool: Practice mindfulness, redirecting negative thoughts and nurturing a constructive mindset.

The practical tool encourages individuals to practice mindfulness, redirecting negative thoughts, and nurturing a constructive mindset. Mindfulness involves being present in the moment, observing thoughts without judgment, and consciously choosing positive perspectives.

Practicing Mindfulness for a Constructive Mindset:

1. Understanding Mindfulness: Mindfulness is the practice of bringing one's attention to the present moment, observing thoughts and feelings without judgment. It involves cultivating awareness and fostering a non-reactive, accepting mindset.

2. Redirecting Negative Thoughts: The tool focuses on redirecting negative thoughts when they arise. Instead of getting entangled in pessimistic or unproductive thinking, mindfulness encourages individuals to acknowledge the thoughts and gently guide their focus toward more constructive perspectives.

How to Implement the Tool:

1. Mindful Breathing: Engage in mindful breathing exercises to anchor yourself in the present moment. Focus on the sensation of

each breath, allowing it to bring your attention away from negative thoughts and into the current experience.

2. Observation Without Judgment: Practice observing your thoughts without judgment. When negative thoughts arise, view them objectively without attaching labels of right or wrong. This non-judgmental awareness creates distance from the thoughts and reduces their impact.

3. Positive Affirmations: Integrate positive affirmations into your mindfulness practice. When negative thoughts emerge, consciously replace them with affirmations that reflect a constructive mindset. Affirmations can counteract negativity and promote a more optimistic outlook.

4. Body Scan Meditation: Incorporate body scan meditation, where you bring attention to different parts of your body. This practice enhances self-awareness and redirects focus from negative thoughts to the physical sensations in the present moment.

5. Mindful Walking: Practice mindful walking, paying attention to each step and the sensations in your body. This form of moving mindfulness can help break the cycle of negative thinking and create a sense of grounding in the present.

Benefits of Practicing Mindfulness:

1. Increased Emotional Regulation: Mindfulness enhances emotional regulation by allowing individuals to observe emotions without immediately reacting. This increased emotional awareness contributes to a more measured and constructive response to challenges.

2. Reduced Stress and Anxiety: Mindfulness is known for its stress-reducing benefits. Redirecting negative thoughts through mindfulness practices helps alleviate stress and anxiety, promoting a calmer and more balanced mental state.

3. Improved Focus and Concentration: Regular mindfulness practice improves focus and concentration. Redirecting negative thoughts allows for better concentration on tasks at hand, fostering a more productive and efficient mindset.

4. Enhanced Self-Awareness: Mindfulness cultivates self-awareness by encouraging individuals to observe their thoughts and reactions. This heightened self-awareness facilitates a deeper understanding of one's mental patterns and paves the way for personal growth.

5. Positive Shift in Perspective: Redirecting negative thoughts through mindfulness leads to a positive shift in perspective. It enables individuals to approach challenges with a more optimistic and solution-oriented mindset, fostering resilience and adaptability.

Adapt to Your Preferences:

1. Mindfulness Apps: Utilize mindfulness apps that offer guided meditation and breathing exercises. These apps provide structured sessions for individuals who prefer guided practices.

2. Mindful Art or Creativity: Engage in mindful art or creative activities as a way to redirect negative thoughts. Activities such as drawing, painting, or crafting can serve as a meditative outlet.

3. Nature Mindfulness: Practice mindfulness in nature. Spend time outdoors, focusing on the sights, sounds, and sensations. Nature

mindfulness can be a powerful way to shift perspective and nurture a positive mindset.

4. Mindful Eating: Apply mindfulness to eating by savoring each bite and being fully present during meals. This practice not only enhances the eating experience but also redirects attention away from negative thoughts.

5. Mindfulness Retreats: Consider participating in mindfulness retreats for more immersive experiences. Retreats provide dedicated time and guidance for deepening mindfulness practices and cultivating a constructive mindset.

By incorporating mindfulness into daily life, individuals can redirect negative thoughts and foster a constructive mindset. This tool empowers individuals to approach challenges with clarity, resilience, and a positive outlook, contributing to overall well-being and personal growth.

53) Embrace Change as a Constant:

Anecdote: Picture a flowing river. Change is as natural as the water's movement.

Interpretation: Adaptability is a strength; resist the urge to cling to the familiar.

Practical Tool: Approach change with an open mind, seeing it as an opportunity for growth.

The practical tool encourages individuals to approach change with an open mind, seeing it as an opportunity for growth. This mindset involves embracing change as a positive force that can lead to personal and professional development.

Approaching Change with an Open Mind:

1. Understanding the Open Mindset: An open mindset involves a willingness to consider new ideas, perspectives, and possibilities. It's a mindset that acknowledges change as a natural part of life and views it as an opportunity for learning and growth rather than a threat.

2. Seeing Change as an Opportunity for Growth: The tool emphasizes viewing change not as a disruption or challenge but as a chance for personal and professional development. It involves recognizing that navigating through changes can lead to enhanced skills, resilience, and a broader understanding of oneself and the world.

How to Implement the Tool:

1. Cultivate Curiosity: Approach change with curiosity and a desire to learn. Ask questions, seek understanding, and explore the possibilities that come with the changes. Cultivating curiosity allows for a more open and receptive mindset.

2. Focus on Learning: Shift your focus from the potential discomfort of change to the opportunities for learning and growth it presents. Consider what skills, insights, or experiences you can gain from the changing circumstances.

3. Adaptability and Flexibility: Develop adaptability and flexibility in your approach to change. Embrace the idea that adaptability is a valuable skill that allows you to navigate uncertainty with resilience and grace.

4. Positive Reframing: Practice positive reframing by consciously interpreting change in a positive light. Instead of dwelling on potential challenges, focus on the positive aspects and opportunities that change brings. This mental shift contributes to a more optimistic perspective.

5. Set Growth Goals: Set specific growth goals in response to change. Identify areas where you can grow personally or professionally as a result of the changing circumstances. Setting growth goals provides direction and purpose during periods of change.

Benefits of Approaching Change with an Open Mind:

1. Continuous Learning: An open mindset toward change fosters a culture of continuous learning. Embracing new situations as opportunities for learning ensures that individuals remain adaptable and receptive to new information and experiences.

2. Enhanced Resilience: Approaching change as an opportunity for growth contributes to enhanced resilience. A mindset that sees challenges as chances to develop resilience enables individuals to bounce back from setbacks more effectively.

3. Increased Creativity: An open mind encourages creativity. When faced with change, individuals with an open mindset are more likely to generate creative solutions and innovative approaches to navigate the new circumstances.

4. Expanded Perspective: Viewing change as an opportunity broadens one's perspective. Embracing change allows individuals to see the bigger picture, understand different viewpoints, and

appreciate the diversity of experiences that come with evolving circumstances.

5. Career and Personal Development: Change often opens doors for career and personal development. Embracing change as a pathway to growth positions individuals to seize new opportunities, take on challenges, and advance in their careers and personal lives.

Adapt to Your Preferences:

1. Change Mindfulness Practices: Incorporate mindfulness practices specifically designed to help individuals navigate change. Mindfulness can promote a calm and centered mindset, making it easier to approach change with openness.

2. Seek Mentorship: Seek mentorship from individuals who have successfully navigated through significant changes. Learning from others' experiences can provide valuable insights and guidance on embracing change with an open mind.

3. Networking and Collaboration: Engage in networking and collaborative activities. Interacting with diverse individuals and working on joint projects can expose you to different perspectives and foster an open-minded approach to change.

4. Reflective Journaling: Maintain a reflective journal where you document your thoughts and feelings about ongoing changes. This practice can help you process emotions, identify areas for growth, and reinforce an open mindset.

5. Celebrate Small Wins: Celebrate small wins and achievements that result from adapting to change. Recognizing and celebrating

progress, no matter how incremental, reinforces a positive and open mindset toward ongoing changes.

By adopting an open mindset and seeing change as an opportunity for growth, individuals can navigate uncertainties with resilience, creativity, and a positive outlook. This tool empowers individuals to embrace change as a natural part of life and leverage it for continuous learning and personal development.

54) Speak Less, Listen More:

Anecdote: Picture a wise elder. Their words carry weight because they choose them carefully.

Interpretation: Listening enhances understanding; thoughtful speech has greater impact.

Practical Tool: Pause before speaking, actively listen to others, and choose words with intention.

The practical tool encourages individuals to pause before speaking, actively listen to others, and choose words with intention. This approach emphasizes the importance of thoughtful communication, fostering better understanding and connection in interactions.

Pause Before Speaking and Choose Words with Intention:

1. Pause for Reflection: The tool begins with the practice of pausing before speaking. This moment of reflection allows individuals to consider the impact of their words, ensuring that communication is intentional rather than impulsive. It provides an opportunity to gather thoughts and choose a response consciously.

2. Active Listening: Active listening is a crucial component of the tool. It involves fully concentrating, understanding, responding,

and remembering what is being said. By actively listening to others, individuals demonstrate respect, empathy, and a genuine interest in the conversation. This creates a foundation for meaningful communication.

3. Choose Words with Intention: The tool encourages individuals to be intentional in their choice of words. Rather than speaking impulsively, individuals should consider the message they want to convey and the impact it may have on the listener. Choosing words with intention involves clarity, sincerity, and alignment with one's values.

How to Implement the Tool:

1. Practice Mindful Communication: Engage in mindful communication by being present in the moment. Avoid multitasking or formulating responses while others are speaking. Instead, focus on the speaker, their message, and the emotions conveyed.

2. Count to Three Before Responding: Implement a simple technique of counting to three before responding. This brief pause allows individuals to collect their thoughts, avoid impulsive reactions, and respond more deliberately.

3. Use Non-Verbal Cues: Utilize non-verbal cues such as nodding, maintaining eye contact, and providing affirming gestures. Non-verbal communication complements spoken words and demonstrates active engagement in the conversation.

4. Reflect on the Message: Take a moment to reflect on the message being communicated. Consider the underlying

emotions, perspectives, and potential nuances. This reflective pause contributes to a more empathetic and thoughtful response.

5. Consider the Impact: Before speaking, consider the potential impact of your words on the listener. Choose language that is respectful, inclusive, and aligned with the message you want to convey. This consideration is especially important in sensitive or challenging conversations.

Benefits of Pausing and Choosing Words with Intention:

1. Improved Communication: Pausing and choosing words with intention leads to improved communication. Clear and thoughtful expression enhances understanding, reducing the likelihood of miscommunication or misunderstandings.

2. Enhanced Connection: Mindful communication fosters a deeper connection with others. Actively listening and choosing words with intention create an environment of mutual respect, empathy, and understanding.

3. Conflict Resolution: The tool is effective in conflict resolution. By pausing, actively listening, and choosing words carefully, individuals can navigate disagreements more effectively, promoting constructive dialogue and resolution.

4. Cultivation of Empathy: The practice encourages the cultivation of empathy. Taking the time to listen actively and choosing words with consideration allows individuals to better understand others' perspectives and respond with empathy.

5. Building Trust: Thoughtful communication contributes to the building of trust. When individuals consistently pause, listen

actively, and choose words intentionally, trust is established as others perceive them as reliable and considerate communicators.

Adapt to Your Preferences:

1. Journaling for Reflection: Incorporate reflective journaling as a practice. After conversations, jot down thoughts and observations about your communication style. This self-reflection enhances awareness and supports continuous improvement.

2. Mindfulness Meditation: Integrate mindfulness meditation into your routine. Mindfulness practices that focus on breath awareness and present-moment attention can enhance your ability to pause and respond thoughtfully in various situations.

3. Communication Workshops: Attend communication workshops or training sessions to develop effective communication skills. These workshops often provide practical tools and strategies for pausing, active listening, and intentional communication.

4. Receive Feedback Gracefully: Foster a mindset of continuous improvement by actively seeking and receiving feedback on your communication style. Use feedback as a guide for refining your approach and further developing your communication skills.

5. Set Communication Intentions: Before engaging in conversations, set intentions for your communication. Consider the tone, message, and desired outcome of your words. Setting intentions helps align your communication with your goals.

By adopting the practice of pausing before speaking, actively listening, and choosing words with intention, individuals can enhance their communication skills. This tool promotes meaningful and respectful interactions, contributing to improved relationships, effective collaboration, and a positive communication environment.

55) Cultivate Resilience in the Face of Adversity:

Anecdote: Imagine a resilient tree in a storm. Bend but don't break in the face of challenges.

Interpretation: Resilience enables you to withstand difficulties and bounce back stronger.

Practical Tool: Develop coping mechanisms, drawing strength from setbacks rather than succumbing to them.

The practical tool encourages individuals to develop coping mechanisms, drawing strength from setbacks rather than succumbing to them. This approach emphasizes resilience and the ability to navigate challenges by finding inner strength and learning from adversity.

Develop Coping Mechanisms and Draw Strength from Setbacks:

1. Understanding Coping Mechanisms: Coping mechanisms are strategies or behaviors individuals use to manage stress, challenges, or difficult emotions. Developing effective coping mechanisms enables individuals to navigate setbacks and adversity with greater resilience.

2. Drawing Strength from Setbacks: The tool emphasizes the mindset of drawing strength from setbacks. Instead of viewing setbacks as insurmountable obstacles, individuals are encouraged to see them as opportunities for growth, learning, and inner strength.

How to Implement the Tool:

1. Identify Personal Coping Strategies: Begin by identifying personal coping strategies that work for you. These could include activities such as mindfulness, exercise, journaling, seeking support from others, or engaging in hobbies. Recognize what helps you navigate stress and setbacks.

2. Build a Support System: Establish a support system of friends, family, or mentors. Having a network of people to lean on during challenging times provides emotional support and different perspectives, contributing to resilience.

3. Learn from Setbacks: Instead of viewing setbacks as failures, approach them as learning experiences. Identify lessons that can be gleaned from the challenges you face. This mindset shift allows setbacks to become stepping stones for personal and professional development.

4. Cultivate a Positive Mindset: Cultivate a positive mindset by focusing on the strengths and skills you possess. Acknowledge your ability to overcome difficulties and the resilience you've demonstrated in the past. Positive self-talk contributes to a more optimistic outlook.

5. Set Realistic Goals: Set realistic and achievable goals, especially during challenging times. Break larger challenges into smaller, more manageable steps. Achieving these smaller goals provides a sense of accomplishment and progress.

Benefits of Developing Coping Mechanisms:

1. Enhanced Resilience: Developing coping mechanisms contributes to enhanced resilience. Individuals who have effective strategies for managing stress and setbacks bounce back more quickly from challenges.

2. Improved Mental Well-Being: Coping mechanisms positively impact mental well-being. Engaging in activities that promote relaxation, mindfulness, or self-reflection fosters emotional well-being, reducing the negative effects of stress.

3. Increased Self-Awareness: The process of developing coping mechanisms enhances self-awareness. Understanding what works for you in times of difficulty allows for a more intentional and proactive approach to managing setbacks.

4. Greater Adaptability: Effective coping mechanisms enhance adaptability. Individuals with well-developed coping strategies can adjust to changing circumstances more easily, maintaining a sense of equilibrium in the face of uncertainty.

5. Empowerment and Control: Developing coping mechanisms empowers individuals to feel more in control of their responses to challenges. Instead of feeling overwhelmed, individuals can take proactive steps to manage stress and setbacks, fostering a sense of empowerment.

Adapt to Your Preferences:

1. Mindfulness Practices: Incorporate mindfulness practices into your routine. Activities such as meditation, deep breathing, or

mindful walking can help center your mind and provide a sense of calm during challenging times.

2. Creative Outlets: Engage in creative outlets as coping mechanisms. Art, music, writing, or other creative expressions can serve as therapeutic tools for processing emotions and finding strength.

3. Professional Support: Seek professional support when needed. Therapists, counselors, or coaches can provide guidance and strategies for coping with setbacks, particularly in situations where additional support is beneficial.

4. Physical Activity: Integrate physical activity into your coping mechanisms. Exercise has numerous mental health benefits, including stress reduction and the release of endorphins that contribute to a positive mood.

5. Reflective Practices: Adopt reflective practices such as journaling. Writing about your experiences, thoughts, and emotions can provide clarity, insights, and a sense of release during challenging times.

By actively developing coping mechanisms and drawing strength from setbacks, individuals can navigate life's challenges with resilience and a positive mindset. This tool encourages a proactive approach to adversity, fostering personal growth and an increased capacity to face future setbacks with strength and determination.

56) Choose Quality Over Quantity in Relationships:

Anecdote: Picture a garden with carefully tended flowers. Nurture deep connections rather than superficial ones.

Interpretation: Meaningful relationships enrich your life more than a multitude of shallow ones.

Practical Tool: Invest time and energy in cultivating a few strong connections, fostering a supportive network.

The practical tool encourages individuals to invest time and energy in cultivating a few strong connections, fostering a supportive network. This approach emphasizes the quality of relationships over quantity and underscores the value of having a reliable and supportive network.

Invest Time and Energy in Cultivating Strong Connections:

1. Quality Over Quantity: The tool prioritizes quality relationships over a large number of superficial connections. Cultivating strong connections involves investing time and effort into nurturing meaningful, supportive, and reciprocal relationships.

2. Foster a Supportive Network: The focus is on building a supportive network of individuals who genuinely care about your well-being and success. A supportive network provides emotional support, encouragement, and a sense of belonging.

How to Implement the Tool:

1. Identify Key Relationships: Begin by identifying key relationships that hold significance in your life. These could include family members, close friends, mentors, or colleagues with whom you share a deep connection.

2. Prioritize Communication: Actively prioritize communication with those in your network. Regular and meaningful conversations help maintain strong connections and allow you to stay informed about each other's lives.

3. Offer Support and Empathy: Be proactive in offering support and empathy to your connections. Show genuine interest in their experiences, listen actively, and provide assistance when needed. A supportive network thrives on reciprocal care and understanding.

4. Celebrate Achievements: Celebrate the achievements and milestones of those in your network. Recognizing and acknowledging each other's successes fosters a positive and uplifting environment within the relationships.

5. Invest Time Together: Spend quality time together, whether in person or virtually. Shared experiences contribute to the depth of connections and create lasting memories. Regularly investing time in each other's company strengthens the bond.

Benefits of Cultivating Strong Connections:

1. Emotional Support: Cultivating strong connections ensures a reliable source of emotional support. During challenging times, having individuals who understand and empathize with your experiences can be invaluable.

2. Sense of Belonging: Strong connections contribute to a sense of belonging. Knowing that you are a valued and integral part of a supportive network enhances feelings of connection and community.

3. Increased Resilience: Supportive relationships bolster resilience. Knowing that you have a network of individuals who stand by you provides the strength and encouragement needed to navigate life's ups and downs.
4. Professional Growth: Strong connections can contribute to professional growth. Mentors, colleagues, or industry peers within your network can provide valuable insights, guidance, and opportunities for career advancement.
5. Enhanced Well-Being: The tool positively impacts overall well-being. Strong connections are associated with improved mental and emotional health, as individuals feel a greater sense of support, understanding, and companionship.

Adapt to Your Preferences:

1. Regular Check-Ins: Incorporate regular check-ins into your routine. This could involve scheduled phone calls, video chats, or face-to-face meetings. Consistent communication helps maintain the strength of your connections.
2. Shared Hobbies or Interests: Explore shared hobbies or interests with individuals in your network. Engaging in activities together creates additional bonding opportunities and strengthens the connection through shared experiences.
3. Networking Events: Attend networking events or gatherings where you can meet like-minded individuals. Building connections within your professional or personal interests expands your network and potential sources of support.
4. Group Activities: Plan and participate in group activities. Whether it's a book club, sports team, or community project,

group activities foster a sense of camaraderie and deepen connections among participants.

5. Virtual Connections: Leverage virtual connections, especially if physical proximity is a challenge. Video calls, online forums, and collaborative projects enable you to cultivate and maintain strong connections across distances.

By intentionally investing time and energy in cultivating a few strong connections, individuals can build a network that offers meaningful support, encouragement, and a sense of community. This tool emphasizes the importance of depth and authenticity in relationships, fostering a strong foundation for personal and professional well-being.

57) Choose Quality Over Quantity in Relationships:

Anecdote: Visualize a gratitude journal. Each entry is a step towards a more positive mindset.

Interpretation: Gratitude shifts your focus from scarcity to abundance.

Practical Tool: Regularly reflect on what you're thankful for, fostering a grateful outlook on life.

The practical tool encourages individuals to regularly reflect on what they're thankful for, fostering a grateful outlook on life. This practice involves acknowledging and appreciating positive aspects of one's life, promoting a mindset of gratitude.

Regularly Reflect on What You're Thankful For:

1. Gratitude as a Daily Practice: The tool advocates for gratitude as a daily practice, encouraging individuals to set aside time

regularly for reflection. This practice involves consciously focusing on and expressing gratitude for positive aspects of one's life.

2. Fostering a Grateful Outlook: The goal is to cultivate a grateful outlook on life by consistently acknowledging and appreciating the blessings, achievements, relationships, and moments of joy that contribute to well-being.

How to Implement the Tool:

1. Establish a Gratitude Routine: Set aside a specific time each day or week to reflect on what you're thankful for. This could be in the morning, before bedtime, or during a designated break. Establishing a routine helps integrate gratitude into your daily life.

2. Keep a Gratitude Journal: Maintain a gratitude journal where you record things you are thankful for regularly. Write down specific moments, people, experiences, or even simple pleasures that bring you joy. The act of journaling reinforces the positive aspects of your life.

3. Express Gratitude to Others: Actively express gratitude to others. This could involve sending thank-you notes, expressing appreciation verbally, or showing kindness to those who contribute positively to your life. Sharing gratitude strengthens connections and spreads positivity.

4. Reflect on Challenges with Gratitude: Practice finding gratitude even in challenging situations. Reflect on the lessons learned, personal growth, or silver linings that may emerge from

difficulties. This perspective shift can turn challenges into opportunities for gratitude.

5. Mindful Appreciation: Be present and mindful in your appreciation. When reflecting on what you're thankful for, immerse yourself in the moment and savor the positive emotions associated with gratitude.

Benefits of Fostering a Grateful Outlook:

1. Positive Mindset: Regular reflection on gratitude contributes to a positive mindset. Acknowledging and appreciating positive aspects of life shifts the focus toward what is going well, fostering optimism.

2. Improved Mental Well-Being: Gratitude practices are linked to improved mental well-being. The act of expressing thanks has been associated with reduced stress, increased happiness, and a greater sense of life satisfaction.

3. Enhanced Relationships: Expressing gratitude to others strengthens relationships. When individuals feel appreciated and valued, it deepens the connection and contributes to a supportive social environment.

4. Resilience in Adversity: A grateful outlook enhances resilience in the face of challenges. Finding gratitude in difficult circumstances provides a coping mechanism and helps individuals navigate adversity with a more positive mindset.

5. Increased Life Satisfaction: Gratitude is correlated with increased life satisfaction. When individuals regularly reflect on what they're thankful for, they tend to experience a greater sense of fulfillment and contentment.

Adapt to Your Preferences:

1. Gratitude Rituals: Incorporate gratitude rituals into your routine. This could include practices such as expressing thanks during meals, incorporating gratitude into your morning or bedtime routine, or using visual cues to prompt reflections on gratitude.

2. Digital Gratitude Reminders: Use digital tools, such as smartphone apps or reminders, to prompt gratitude reflections. Set periodic reminders to pause and reflect on what you're thankful for, especially during busy days.

3. Gratitude Partner: Engage in gratitude reflections with a partner or friend. Sharing what you're thankful for with someone else creates a supportive and collaborative environment for fostering gratitude.

4. Seasonal Reflections: Align gratitude reflections with seasons or specific life events. For example, reflect on what you're thankful for at the end of each month, during holidays, or on significant personal milestones.

5. Gratitude Challenges: Participate in gratitude challenges. These can involve setting goals to express gratitude to a certain number of people each week or finding a specific number of things to be thankful for daily.

By incorporating regular reflections on gratitude into daily life, individuals can cultivate a positive and appreciative outlook. This tool promotes mindfulness, positivity, and an increased awareness of the positive aspects that contribute to a fulfilling and meaningful life.

58) Find Joy in the Journey, Not Just the Destination:

Anecdote: Picture a road trip. The memorable moments are often the unexpected detours.

Interpretation: Enjoy the process of achieving goals; it's not just about reaching the endpoint.

Practical Tool: Celebrate small victories along the way, finding fulfillment in the journey.

The practical tool encourages individuals to celebrate small victories along the way, finding fulfillment in the journey. This approach emphasizes the importance of acknowledging and appreciating incremental achievements, fostering a positive and fulfilling mindset throughout the journey toward larger goals.

Celebrate Small Victories Along the Way:

1. Recognition of Incremental Achievements: The tool advocates for the recognition of incremental achievements, urging individuals to celebrate small victories rather than solely focusing on the end goal. This practice acknowledges the progress made throughout the journey.

2. Finding Fulfillment in the Journey: The emphasis is on deriving fulfillment from the process and experiences along the way, rather than waiting for a specific outcome. Celebrating small victories contributes to a positive mindset and a sense of accomplishment.

How to Implement the Tool:

1. Define Milestones: Break down larger goals into smaller, manageable milestones. Each milestone represents a step forward

in the journey. Clearly defining these smaller achievements makes it easier to recognize and celebrate them.

2. Acknowledge Effort and Progress: Acknowledge and celebrate the effort put into the journey, not just the final results. Recognize the progress made, the lessons learned, and the commitment shown along the way. This practice fosters a growth mindset.

3. Create a Celebration Ritual: Develop a ritual for celebrating small victories. This could involve treating yourself to a small reward, sharing the achievement with others, or taking a moment for personal reflection. Rituals reinforce the significance of the accomplishment.

4. Share Achievements with Others: Share your achievements with friends, family, or colleagues. Celebrating with others not only magnifies the joy but also strengthens social connections. Sharing creates a positive and supportive environment.

5. Maintain a Positive Perspective: Cultivate a positive perspective by focusing on what has been achieved rather than what is yet to be done. Regularly reflect on the journey and acknowledge the positive aspects, reinforcing a mindset of gratitude and optimism.

Benefits of Celebrating Small Victories:

1. Motivation and Encouragement: Celebrating small victories provides motivation and encouragement. Recognizing progress boosts morale, encourages perseverance, and reinforces the belief that effort leads to positive outcomes.

2. Increased Confidence: Acknowledging small victories contributes to increased confidence. Recognizing one's ability to

overcome challenges and achieve goals incrementally builds a sense of self-efficacy.

3. Positive Reinforcement: Celebrations serve as positive reinforcement. When individuals associate effort with positive emotions and rewards, it strengthens the connection between hard work and the sense of accomplishment.

4. Enhanced Focus on Process: Celebrating small victories shifts the focus from the end result to the process. Emphasizing the journey fosters a more mindful and present mindset, allowing individuals to savor the experiences along the way.

5. Resilience in the Face of Challenges: Recognizing small victories builds resilience. When faced with challenges, individuals who have developed the habit of celebrating incremental achievements are more likely to maintain a positive outlook and persevere.

Adapt to Your Preferences:

1. Visual Progress Tracking: Use visual tools to track progress. Charts, graphs, or visual representations can serve as a tangible reminder of achievements, making it easier to celebrate and stay motivated.

2. Personal Reflections: Engage in personal reflections on a regular basis. Journaling or creating a diary allows you to document achievements, lessons learned, and moments of joy along the journey.

3. Team Celebrations: If working within a team or community, incorporate collective celebrations. Recognizing group achievements fosters a sense of camaraderie and shared success.

4. Reward Systems: Establish a personal reward system tied to achievements. Small treats, experiences, or activities can serve as rewards for reaching milestones, reinforcing the positive association with progress.

5. Incorporate Mindfulness Practices: Integrate mindfulness practices into the celebration process. Take a moment to mindfully acknowledge and appreciate the accomplishment, allowing the positive emotions to be fully experienced.

By celebrating small victories along the way, individuals can cultivate a positive and resilient mindset. This tool promotes a healthy and fulfilling approach to goal pursuit, encouraging individuals to find joy in the journey and recognize the value of progress, no matter how small.

59) Master the Art of Letting Go:

Anecdote: Picture a balloon released into the sky. Clinging to the string keeps you grounded; releasing it brings freedom.

Interpretation: Letting go of attachments frees you from unnecessary burdens.

Practical Tool: Identify what no longer serves you, whether it's possessions, relationships, or beliefs, and release them.

The practical tool encourages individuals to identify what no longer serves them, whether it's possessions, relationships, or beliefs and to release them. This approach emphasizes the importance of letting go of elements in life that hinder personal growth, well-being, or alignment with one's values.

Identify and Release What No Longer Serves You:

1. Conscious Assessment: The tool advocates for a conscious and thorough assessment of various aspects of life, including possessions, relationships, and beliefs. This involves reflecting on whether these elements contribute positively to personal well-being and growth.

2. Letting Go: The emphasis is on the process of letting go. This could involve decluttering physical spaces, distancing oneself from toxic relationships, or challenging and evolving beliefs that no longer align with personal values and aspirations.

How to Implement the Tool:

1. Inventory of Possessions: Conduct an inventory of possessions, evaluating each item's significance and contribution to your life. Identify items that no longer bring joy, have practical use, or align with your current lifestyle. Declutter and release what is no longer essential.

2. Evaluate Relationships: Evaluate the relationships in your life, considering their impact on your well-being and personal growth. Identify relationships that are toxic, draining, or no longer serve a positive purpose. Create boundaries or, if necessary, distance yourself from relationships that hinder your growth.

3. Examine Beliefs and Mindsets: Reflect on your beliefs, values, and mindset. Identify beliefs that may be limiting, outdated, or no longer resonate with your current understanding of the world. Challenge and evolve these beliefs to align with your personal growth and aspirations.

4. Regular Check-Ins: Implement regular check-ins to assess various aspects of your life. This practice ensures ongoing awareness of what serves you and what doesn't. Regular evaluations allow for continuous refinement and adjustment.

5. Mindful Release: Practice mindful release when letting go of possessions, relationships, or beliefs. Acknowledge the emotions associated with the process and allow yourself to embrace the positive changes that come from releasing what no longer serves you.

Benefits of Identifying and Releasing:

1. Enhanced Well-Being: Letting go of what no longer serves you contributes to enhanced well-being. Removing sources of negativity or stagnation creates space for positive energy, growth, and overall contentment.

2. Clarity and Focus: The tool promotes clarity and focus by decluttering various aspects of life. Removing distractions and unnecessary elements allows for a more focused and intentional approach to personal and professional endeavors.

3. Personal Growth: Identifying and releasing what no longer serves you is a catalyst for personal growth. It creates room for new experiences, opportunities, and perspectives that align with your evolving self.

4. Positive Relationships: Releasing toxic or unfulfilling relationships paves the way for positive and supportive connections. Embracing healthier relationships contributes to emotional well-being and a more positive social environment.

5. Alignment with Values: The tool encourages alignment with personal values. Releasing possessions, relationships, or beliefs that no longer align with your values ensures that your life is in harmony with what truly matters to you.

Adapt to Your Preferences:

1. Gradual Progress: Implement changes gradually. You don't need to overhaul every aspect of your life at once. Gradual progress allows for a more manageable and sustainable transition.
2. Seek Professional Guidance: Seek guidance from professionals, such as therapists or life coaches, when addressing complex issues. Professional support can provide insights and strategies for navigating challenging aspects of the release process.
3. Celebrate Positive Changes: Celebrate the positive changes that come from letting go. Acknowledge the growth, liberation, and newfound opportunities that arise as a result of releasing what no longer serves you.
4. Create a Vision Board: Use visual tools like a vision board to represent your aspirations and values. This can serve as a reminder of the direction you want to move toward, making it easier to identify and release elements that deviate from that vision.
5. Engage in Self-Reflection: Regularly engage in self-reflection to deepen your understanding of your evolving self. Periodic introspection ensures that you remain in tune with your changing needs and aspirations.

By consciously identifying and releasing what no longer serves you, individuals can create a space for positive transformation, personal growth, and a life that is more aligned with their values and aspirations. This tool emphasizes the importance of intentional living and ongoing self-awareness.

60) Balance Ambition With Contentment:

Anecdote: Imagine a scale with ambition on one side and contentment on the other. Balance is the key.

Interpretation: Strive for success while appreciating what you have in the present.

Practical Tool: Set ambitious goals but take time to savor and be content with your current achievements.

The practical tool encourages individuals to set ambitious goals but also emphasizes the importance of taking time to savor and be content with current achievements. This approach seeks to strike a balance between striving for continuous improvement and recognizing and appreciating the successes already attained.

Set Ambitious Goals and Savor Current Achievements:

1. Ambitious Goal Setting: The tool promotes the setting of ambitious and challenging goals. These goals should be aspirational, inspiring individuals to reach beyond their current capabilities and strive for significant accomplishments.

2. Strive for Continuous Improvement: Emphasis is placed on the idea of continuous improvement. Ambitious goals serve as a driving force for personal and professional development, pushing individuals to grow, learn, and achieve at higher levels.

3. Celebrate Current Achievements: In addition to striving for future goals, the tool highlights the importance of acknowledging

and celebrating current achievements. This involves taking time to savor the successes and recognizing the progress made along the way.

How to Implement the Tool:

1. Define Ambitious Goals: Clearly define ambitious goals that challenge and inspire you. These goals should stretch your abilities and push you beyond your comfort zone, fostering personal and professional growth.

2. Break Goals into Milestones: Break down ambitious goals into smaller, manageable milestones. This step-by-step approach makes the larger objectives more achievable and allows for the celebration of progress along the way.

3. Regular Reflection: Engage in regular reflection on both your current achievements and your long-term goals. Reflecting on accomplishments provides a sense of fulfillment and motivates continued progress toward ambitious objectives.

4. Savor Successes Mindfully: Practice mindfulness when savoring current achievements. Take the time to fully appreciate and relish the successes, acknowledging the hard work, dedication, and effort that contributed to reaching those milestones.

5. Express Gratitude: Express gratitude for the achievements, recognizing the support, opportunities, and resources that have played a role in your success. Gratitude fosters a positive mindset and enhances the overall experience of achievement.

Benefits of Setting Ambitious Goals and Savoring Achievements:

1. Motivation for Growth: Ambitious goals serve as powerful motivators for personal and professional growth. The pursuit of

challenging objectives keeps individuals engaged, enthusiastic, and continuously striving for improvement.

2. Increased Resilience: Striving for ambitious goals builds resilience. The challenges encountered in pursuit of high-level achievements contribute to the development of resilience and the ability to overcome obstacles.

3. Enhanced Self-Efficacy: Achieving ambitious goals enhances self-efficacy—the belief in one's ability to succeed. Successes, both big and small, contribute to a positive self-perception and the confidence to tackle even more significant challenges.

4. Satisfaction and Fulfillment: Savoring and celebrating current achievements bring satisfaction and fulfillment. Taking the time to appreciate successes provides a sense of accomplishment and contributes to overall well-being.

5. Balanced Perspective: The tool promotes a balanced perspective on achievement. While ambitious goals drive progress, savoring current successes ensures that individuals maintain a healthy and positive outlook, avoiding burnout or dissatisfaction.

Adapt to Your Preferences:

1. Personalize Goal-Setting Process: Tailor the goal-setting process to your personal preferences and values. Align ambitious goals with your passions and aspirations to make the journey more meaningful.

2. Collaborate and Share Successes: Collaborate with others in setting and achieving ambitious goals. Sharing successes and celebrating achievements with a supportive network enhances the sense of accomplishment.

3. Mindful Practices: Incorporate mindfulness practices into your routine. Mindful reflection and appreciation of achievements contribute to a deeper and more meaningful experience of success.
4. Reward Systems: Establish personal reward systems for achieving milestones. Celebrate achievements with small rewards that reinforce the positive connection between effort and success.
5. Periodic Goal Review: Periodically review and reassess your ambitious goals. Adjustments may be necessary based on changing circumstances or evolving priorities. This adaptive approach ensures that goals remain relevant and achievable.

By setting ambitious goals and consciously savoring and celebrating current achievements, individuals can maintain a healthy and balanced approach to personal and professional growth. This tool encourages a mindset that appreciates both the journey and the destination, fostering a fulfilling and sustainable path to success.

61) Be Mindful of Your Inner Dialogue:

Anecdote: Picture a mirror reflecting your thoughts. Your self-talk shapes your self-perception.

Interpretation: Pay attention to the tone of your inner dialogue; be a supportive voice to yourself.

Practical Tool: Challenge negative self-talk, replacing it with affirmations and constructive thoughts.

The practical tool encourages individuals to challenge negative self-talk and replace it with affirmations and constructive thoughts. This approach aims to promote a positive mindset, self-empowerment, and improved mental well-being.

Challenge Negative Self-Talk and Replace with Affirmations:

1. Awareness of Negative Self-Talk: The tool begins with cultivating awareness of negative self-talk. This involves recognizing and acknowledging the critical or pessimistic thoughts that may arise in one's internal dialogue.

2. Questioning and Challenging Thoughts: Individuals are encouraged to question and challenge negative thoughts. This involves examining the validity of these thoughts, considering alternative perspectives, and assessing whether they are based on facts or unfounded assumptions.

3. Affirmations as Positive Counterstatements: Affirmations serve as positive counterstatements to negative self-talk. These are empowering, uplifting, and constructive statements that individuals repeat to themselves to reinforce positive beliefs and foster a more optimistic mindset.

How to Implement the Tool:

1. Self-Observation: Pay attention to your thoughts and self-talk throughout the day. Practice self-observation to identify instances of negative or self-critical thinking. Journaling can be a helpful tool for recording and analyzing these thoughts.

2. Question Negative Thoughts: When negative thoughts arise, question their validity. Challenge assumptions and ask yourself if

there is evidence supporting these thoughts. Consider whether the thoughts are based on past experiences or irrational fears.

3. Positive Affirmations: Develop a set of positive affirmations that counteract specific negative beliefs. Affirmations should be personalized and focus on strengths, capabilities, and positive qualities. Repeat these affirmations regularly, especially during moments of self-doubt.

4. Visualization Techniques: Use visualization techniques to accompany affirmations. Picture yourself succeeding, achieving goals, and overcoming challenges. Visualization reinforces the positive messages conveyed by affirmations.

5. Mindfulness Practices: Incorporate mindfulness practices to stay present and observe your thoughts without judgment. Mindfulness allows you to create space between negative self-talk and your response, enabling a more intentional and positive mindset.

Benefits of Challenging Negative Self-Talk:

1. Improved Mental Health: Challenging negative self-talk contributes to improved mental health. By reframing negative thoughts, individuals can reduce stress, anxiety, and feelings of inadequacy, fostering a more positive emotional state.

2. Enhanced Self-Esteem: Addressing negative self-talk is linked to enhanced self-esteem. Affirmations and constructive thoughts reinforce a positive self-perception, leading to greater confidence and self-worth.

3. Increased Resilience: Individuals who challenge negative self-talk develop increased resilience. By reframing challenges as

opportunities for growth and learning, they are better equipped to navigate setbacks and bounce back from adversity.

4. Positive Mindset: The tool promotes the cultivation of a positive mindset. Replacing negative self-talk with affirmations helps shift the overall cognitive outlook, fostering optimism and a belief in one's ability to overcome challenges.

5. Empowerment and Self-Empathy: Challenging negative self-talk empowers individuals to take control of their thoughts and emotions. It encourages self-empathy, allowing individuals to treat themselves with the same kindness and understanding they would offer to others.

Adapt to Your Preferences:

1. Create Personalized Affirmations: Tailor affirmations to your specific needs and goals. Personalized affirmations are more impactful and resonate on a deeper level, addressing your unique challenges and aspirations.

2. Affirmation Journal: Maintain an affirmation journal where you regularly write down positive affirmations. This creates a tangible record of your empowering thoughts and serves as a reminder of your strengths and capabilities.

3. Use Positive Language: Integrate positive language into your self-talk. Pay attention to the words you use when thinking about yourself and consciously replace negative language with affirming and constructive words.

4. Affirmation Practices in Routine: Incorporate affirmation practices into your daily routine. Repeat affirmations during

morning rituals, before significant tasks, or as part of relaxation exercises. Consistency enhances the effectiveness of this tool.

5. Seek Support and Feedback: Share your affirmations with a trusted friend, mentor, or therapist. Seeking support and feedback can provide additional perspectives and encouragement, reinforcing the positive impact of challenging negative self-talk.

By actively challenging negative self-talk and replacing it with affirmations and constructive thoughts, individuals can cultivate a more positive and empowering mindset. This tool empowers individuals to reshape their internal dialogue, promoting mental well-being and resilience in the face of life's challenges.

62) Cherish Moments of Solitude:

Anecdote: Imagine a quiet forest. Solitude is a sanctuary for self-discovery and reflection.

Interpretation: Time alone allows for introspection and personal growth..

Practical Tool: Schedule moments of solitude to recharge and connect with your inner self.

The practical tool encourages individuals to schedule moments of solitude to recharge and connect with their inner selves. This approach recognizes the importance of taking intentional breaks from external stimuli to foster self-reflection, relaxation, and overall well-being.

Schedule Moments of Solitude to Recharge and Connect:

1. Intentional Planning: The tool emphasizes the intentional scheduling of moments of solitude. This involves proactively

setting aside dedicated time in your schedule for solitary activities that allow you to recharge and connect with your inner self.

2. Disconnecting from External Stimuli: During these scheduled moments, individuals are encouraged to disconnect from external stimuli such as electronic devices, social media, and other distractions. This intentional disconnect creates a space for inner reflection and mental rejuvenation.

3. Engaging in Self-Reflective Activities: Solitary moments are an opportunity to engage in self-reflective activities. This could include journaling, meditation, deep breathing exercises, or simply being present in the moment without external pressures.

How to Implement the Tool:

1. Identify Solitude Preferences: Determine the types of activities that bring you a sense of calm and introspection. Whether it's reading, walking in nature, or practicing mindfulness, identify solitude preferences that resonate with you.

2. Block Dedicated Time in Your Schedule: Actively block specific time slots in your schedule for moments of solitude. Treat these appointments with the same importance as any other commitment, ensuring that you prioritize your well-being and inner connection.

3. Create a Quiet Environment: Choose environments that facilitate solitude and quietness. Whether it's a peaceful corner in your home, a quiet park, or a cozy library, select spaces that allow you to disconnect from external noise and distractions.

4. Disconnect from Digital Devices: During your moments of solitude, disconnect from digital devices. Turn off notifications, put your phone on silent, or consider leaving it behind altogether. This intentional break from technology enhances the depth of your solitary experience.
5. Engage in Mindful Activities: Engage in activities that promote mindfulness and self-awareness. This could involve practices like meditation, deep breathing, or simply sitting in quiet contemplation. Allow your mind to wander and explore your thoughts without external pressures.

Benefits of Scheduling Moments of Solitude:
1. Stress Reduction: Scheduled solitude provides a break from the demands of daily life, contributing to stress reduction. It allows the mind to unwind, promoting relaxation and a sense of calm.
2. Enhanced Creativity and Clarity: Solitude fosters enhanced creativity and mental clarity. Time spent alone allows for deeper introspection and the generation of new ideas without external influences.
3. Improved Self-Awareness: Engaging in self-reflective activities during moments of solitude promotes improved self-awareness. Individuals can gain deeper insights into their emotions, thoughts, and values, fostering personal growth.
4. Recharged Energy Levels: Solitude acts as a recharging mechanism for energy levels. Taking a break from constant engagement with others and external stimuli helps replenish mental and emotional energy.

5. Greater Emotional Resilience: Regularly scheduling moments of solitude contributes to greater emotional resilience. It provides individuals with the space to process emotions, navigate challenges, and build inner strength.

Adapt to Your Preferences:

1. Explore Various Solitude Activities: Experiment with different solitude activities to discover what resonates with you. Whether it's reading, practicing yoga, or spending time in nature, tailor the experience to your preferences.

2. Combine Solitude with Hobbies: Combine moments of solitude with activities you enjoy as hobbies. This could include painting, playing a musical instrument, or engaging in any creative pursuit that brings you joy and relaxation.

3. Flexible Scheduling: Be flexible with your scheduling approach. While some individuals may prefer regular daily moments of solitude, others may find that longer, less frequent breaks better suit their needs. Adapt the scheduling to align with your lifestyle.

4. Solo Retreats: Consider planning solo retreats or day trips for extended periods of solitude. This could involve getting away to a quiet place, disconnecting from routine, and immersing yourself in self-reflective practices.

5. Incorporate Reflection into Daily Routines: If daily solitude seems challenging, incorporate reflective moments into your existing routine. This could be as simple as taking a few mindful breaths before starting your day or reflecting on the day's events before bedtime.

By intentionally scheduling moments of solitude, individuals can cultivate a deeper connection with their inner selves, promoting mental well-being, and creating a foundation for personal growth and self-discovery. This tool encourages a conscious balance between engagement with the external world and nurturing one's internal landscape.

63) Practice Humility in Success:

Anecdote: Picture a humble leader. Success doesn't diminish their humility; it enhances it.

Interpretation: Achievements are best appreciated with a humble heart.

Practical Tool: Acknowledge your successes with gratitude, attributing them to a combination of effort and external factors. The practical tool encourages individuals to acknowledge their successes with gratitude, attributing them to a combination of personal effort and external factors. This approach emphasizes the importance of recognizing and appreciating one's achievements while acknowledging the contributions of external elements that played a role.

Acknowledge Successes with Gratitude:

1. Reflection on Achievements: The tool begins with encouraging individuals to reflect on their achievements, both big and small. This involves a conscious awareness of the positive outcomes and accomplishments in various aspects of life.

2. Gratitude Practice: Individuals are prompted to cultivate a sense of gratitude for their successes. This involves expressing

appreciation for the opportunities, support, resources, and circumstances that contributed to the achievement of their goals.

3. Attribution to Effort and External Factors: The tool advocates for a balanced attribution of success to both personal effort and external factors. Rather than solely focusing on individual achievements, individuals are encouraged to recognize the collaborative influence of internal and external elements.

How to Implement the Tool:

1. Celebrate Achievements Mindfully: When celebrating achievements, do so mindfully. Take the time to acknowledge and savor the success. Express gratitude for the effort you invested, recognizing the hard work, dedication, and perseverance that led to the positive outcome.

2. Express Gratitude for External Factors: Identify and express gratitude for external factors that played a role in your success. This could include supportive relationships, opportunities that came your way, mentorship, or favorable circumstances. Recognize the interconnectedness of personal effort and external contributions.

3. Avoid Undermining Personal Effort: While acknowledging external factors, avoid undermining your personal effort. Recognize the skills, abilities, and commitment you brought to the table. This balanced perspective fosters a healthy sense of self-worth and confidence.

4. Gratitude Journaling: Consider keeping a gratitude journal to regularly document and reflect on your successes. Write down the specific achievements, the effort you invested, and the

external factors that contributed. This practice reinforces a positive mindset.

5. Share Successes with Others: Share your successes with others and express gratitude for their support and involvement. This could be friends, family, colleagues, or mentors. Sharing successes enhances the sense of community and reinforces the collaborative nature of achievement.

Benefits of Acknowledging Successes with Gratitude:

1. Positive Mindset: Acknowledging successes with gratitude contributes to a positive mindset. Gratitude shifts the focus from what may be lacking to appreciating the abundance of opportunities and support that contribute to success.

2. Improved Well-Being: Expressing gratitude for achievements is linked to improved emotional well-being. It fosters a sense of fulfillment, satisfaction, and contentment, contributing to overall happiness.

3. Enhanced Resilience: Recognizing the combined influence of personal effort and external factors enhances resilience. It encourages individuals to view challenges as opportunities for growth, knowing that both internal and external resources can contribute to overcoming obstacles.

4. Strengthened Relationships: Expressing gratitude for external factors often involves acknowledging the role of others in your success. This strengthens relationships, fostering a supportive network that contributes positively to personal and professional endeavors.

5. Balanced Self-Perception: A balanced attribution of success encourages a healthy self-perception. Individuals recognize their capabilities and contributions while appreciating the interconnectedness with external elements, leading to a more realistic and positive self-image.

Adapt to Your Preferences:

1. Gratitude Rituals: Incorporate gratitude rituals into your routine. Whether it's starting or ending the day with a moment of reflection, establishing consistent practices reinforces the habit of acknowledging successes with gratitude.
2. Visual Reminders: Use visual reminders, such as a vision board or quotes, to reinforce the importance of gratitude in your approach to success. Visual cues serve as prompts for cultivating a thankful mindset.
3. Customize Gratitude Expressions: Customize how you express gratitude. Whether through verbal affirmations, written notes, or acts of kindness, choose expressions that resonate with your personal style and preferences.
4. Reflect on Challenges Overcome: Extend gratitude to the challenges you've overcome. Recognize the lessons learned, growth experienced, and resilience built through navigating obstacles. Gratitude for challenges reframes them as opportunities for development.
5. Integrate Gratitude into Goal Setting: Integrate expressions of gratitude into your goal-setting process. When setting new goals, reflect on past achievements with gratitude. This positive reflection can inspire and motivate you for future endeavors.

By acknowledging successes with gratitude and recognizing the collaboration of personal effort and external factors, individuals can cultivate a positive and appreciative mindset. This tool fosters a holistic approach to achievement, emphasizing the interconnected nature of individual endeavors and the external support that contributes to success.

64) Learn to Differentiate Between Wants and Needs:

Anecdote: Picture a traveler packing for a journey. Needs are essentials; wants are extras.

Interpretation: Distinguish between what is necessary for your well-being and what is simply desirable.

Practical Tool: Before acquiring something, ask if it fulfills a genuine need or if it's just a fleeting want.

The practical tool encourages individuals to consider the necessity of acquiring something by asking whether it fulfills a genuine need or if it's merely a fleeting want. This approach promotes mindful and intentional consumption, helping individuals make more conscious decisions about the items they bring into their lives.

Before Acquiring, Assess Genuine Need vs. Fleeting Want:

1. Mindful Consideration: The tool advocates for a pause and deliberate consideration before acquiring any item. Instead of impulsive or compulsive buying, individuals are encouraged to take a moment to reflect on the actual necessity of the item.

2. Distinguishing Between Need and Want: Individuals are prompted to distinguish between genuine needs and fleeting wants. A genuine need fulfills a necessary function or

requirement, while a fleeting want is often driven by momentary desires, trends, or external influences.

3. Questioning Motivations: The tool encourages individuals to question their motivations for acquiring a particular item. Are they acquiring it out of genuine necessity, or is it driven by external pressures, societal expectations, or momentary impulses?

How to Implement the Tool:

1. Define Genuine Needs: Clearly define what constitutes a genuine need in your life. Genuine needs are items or resources that contribute to your well-being, fulfill essential functions, or align with your core values and priorities.

2. Create a Checklist: Develop a checklist or set of questions to ask yourself before making a purchase. This could include inquiries such as, "Is this item necessary for my daily life?" or "Will acquiring this contribute positively to my long-term goals?"

3. Assess Long-Term Impact: Consider the long-term impact of acquiring the item. Reflect on whether it aligns with your values, contributes positively to your life, and has a lasting purpose beyond immediate gratification.

4. Practice Delayed Gratification: Introduce the practice of delayed gratification. If you identify a desire to acquire something, give yourself time before making the purchase. This delay allows for reflection, helping you assess whether the item is genuinely needed or just a fleeting want.

5. Budget and Prioritize: Establish a budget and prioritize your spending based on genuine needs. Allocate resources to items

that align with your essential requirements and long-term objectives, minimizing impulsive purchases driven by momentary wants.

Benefits of Assessing Genuine Needs vs. Fleeting Wants:

1. Financial Well-Being: By distinguishing between genuine needs and fleeting wants, individuals can make more informed financial decisions. This promotes financial well-being, preventing unnecessary expenditures and fostering responsible budgeting.

2. Reduced Clutter: Mindful acquisition based on genuine needs contributes to a decluttered living space. It prevents the accumulation of unnecessary items that may clutter the home and lead to a more organized and peaceful environment.

3. Increased Contentment: Focusing on genuine needs over fleeting wants contributes to increased contentment. Individuals are more likely to find satisfaction in their possessions when they align with their values and fulfill essential functions.

4. Environmental Impact: Mindful consumption has positive environmental implications. It reduces the demand for unnecessary production, minimizing resource use and waste generation associated with the creation and disposal of non-essential items.

5. Improved Decision-Making: Implementing this tool hones decision-making skills. Individuals become adept at assessing the relevance of an item to their lives, making choices that align with their values and contribute to their overall well-being.

Adapt to Your Preferences:

1. Customize Your Checklist: Tailor the checklist of questions to align with your personal values, lifestyle, and priorities. Customizing the questions makes the tool more relevant to your specific circumstances.

2. Practice Minimalism: Embrace principles of minimalism by focusing on the essentials and reducing excess possessions. This philosophy aligns with the idea of acquiring items based on genuine needs rather than excessive wants.

3. Set Spending Guidelines: Establish guidelines for spending based on genuine needs. This could involve setting a threshold for discretionary spending and evaluating whether potential purchases meet the criteria of necessity.

4. Evaluate Purchase Frequency: Reflect on your overall purchase frequency. If you find yourself acquiring items frequently, assess whether they genuinely contribute to your well-being or if you're succumbing to impulsive buying habits.

5. Monitor Emotional Triggers: Be aware of emotional triggers that may influence impulsive buying. If you sense an emotional impulse driving a purchase, take extra caution and apply the tool to assess the genuine need behind the desire.

By incorporating this tool into decision-making processes, individuals can foster a more intentional and mindful approach to acquiring possessions. This practice not only contributes to financial prudence but also aligns with sustainability, minimalism, and a more contented lifestyle based on genuine needs.

65) Strive for Inner Harmony:

Anecdote: Imagine a symphony. Inner harmony is the melody of balanced emotions and thoughts.

Interpretation: Balance your inner world to navigate life with greater ease.

Practical Tool: Regularly assess your emotional and mental state, adjusting as needed to maintain inner harmony.

The practical tool encourages individuals to regularly assess their emotional and mental state and make adjustments as needed to maintain inner harmony. This approach emphasizes the importance of self-awareness and proactive self-care for overall well-being.

Regularly Assess Emotional and Mental State:

1. Self-Reflection Practices: The tool suggests incorporating self-reflection practices into your routine. This involves taking time to introspect and become aware of your emotional and mental state. Journaling, mindfulness meditation, or simply sitting in quiet contemplation are examples of self-reflection practices.

2. Emotional Check-Ins: Regularly check in with your emotions throughout the day. Assess how you're feeling at different moments and identify any patterns or triggers that may be influencing your emotional state. This self-awareness is crucial for making informed adjustments.

3. Identify Stressors: Recognize potential stressors in your life, whether they are related to work, relationships, or other aspects. Identifying stressors helps you understand their impact on your mental and emotional well-being.

Adjust as Needed to Maintain Inner Harmony:

1. Mindful Responses: Practice mindful responses to your emotions. Instead of reacting impulsively, take a moment to observe and understand your feelings. This mindful approach allows you to choose intentional and constructive responses, contributing to inner harmony.

2. Self-Care Strategies: Develop a repertoire of self-care strategies that align with your needs. This could include activities such as exercise, spending time in nature, engaging in hobbies, or connecting with loved ones. Implement these strategies when needed to restore balance.

3. Set Boundaries: Establish healthy boundaries in various aspects of your life. This includes setting limits on work hours, being mindful of personal space, and managing commitments. Setting boundaries contributes to a sense of control and balance, fostering inner harmony.

4. Prioritize Mental Health: Prioritize your mental health by seeking professional support when needed. If you find persistent challenges or difficulties in maintaining inner harmony, consider consulting with a mental health professional for guidance and assistance.

How to Implement the Tool:

1. Daily Emotional Check-Ins: Set aside time each day for a brief emotional check-in. This could be a few minutes of self-reflection in the morning or evening. Ask yourself how you're feeling emotionally and mentally and note any shifts or patterns.

2. Journaling for Self-Reflection: Use journaling as a tool for self-reflection. Write down your thoughts, emotions, and any events that may have influenced your mental state. Regular journaling provides a tangible record of your emotional journey.

3. Mindfulness Meditation: Incorporate mindfulness meditation into your routine. Mindful breathing and meditation practices help bring awareness to the present moment, allowing you to observe your thoughts and emotions without judgment.

4. Create a Self-Care Plan: Develop a personalized self-care plan that includes activities and strategies to address your emotional and mental well-being. This plan can be tailored to your preferences and can be adjusted as needed.

5. Regular Review of Boundaries: Periodically review and reassess your boundaries. Ensure that your boundaries align with your current needs and circumstances. Adjustments may be necessary based on changes in workload, relationships, or personal priorities.

Benefits of Regularly Assessing and Adjusting:

1. Improved Emotional Regulation: Regular assessment and adjustment contribute to improved emotional regulation. Being aware of your emotions allows you to respond to them in a balanced and constructive manner.

2. Increased Resilience: Proactively addressing stressors and adjusting your approach enhances resilience. You become better equipped to navigate challenges, adapting to changing circumstances while maintaining inner equilibrium.

3. Enhanced Self-Awareness: Regular assessment fosters enhanced self-awareness. Understanding your emotional and mental state allows you to make informed decisions and align your actions with your overall well-being.

4. Prevention of Burnout: Consistent self-assessment helps prevent burnout by identifying signs of excessive stress early on. Adjusting your approach and implementing self-care strategies can mitigate the risk of burnout.

5. Greater Life Satisfaction: Maintaining inner harmony contributes to greater life satisfaction. When you actively assess and address your emotional and mental needs, you create a foundation for a more fulfilling and balanced life.

Adapt to Your Preferences:

1. Customize Self-Care Practices: Customize your self-care practices to suit your preferences. Whether it's spending time in nature, engaging in creative pursuits, or practicing mindfulness, choose activities that resonate with you.

2. Flexible Check-In Times: Be flexible with the times you conduct emotional check-ins. Some individuals may prefer morning reflections, while others may find evening assessments more fitting. Choose times that align with your natural rhythms.

3. Collaborate on Boundaries: If applicable, collaborate with others on setting and respecting boundaries. Communicate openly with colleagues, friends, or family members to ensure that everyone's needs and boundaries are considered.

4. Periodic Goal Review: Periodically review your goals and aspirations. Ensure that your pursuits align with your values and

contribute positively to your mental and emotional well-being. Adjust goals as needed to maintain inner harmony.

5. Experiment with Mindfulness Techniques: Explore various mindfulness techniques to find what works best for you. This could include mindfulness meditation, mindful breathing exercises, or mindful movement practices. Experiment with different approaches to discover what resonates most.

By regularly assessing your emotional and mental state and making adjustments as needed, you cultivate a proactive and intentional approach to inner harmony. This tool empowers individuals to prioritize their well-being, respond effectively to challenges, and maintain a balanced and fulfilling life.

66) Express Love and Appreciation:

Anecdote: Picture a garden blooming with gratitude. Expressing love and appreciation nurtures relationships.

Interpretation: Verbalizing affection strengthens connections and uplifts others.

Practical Tool: Regularly express love and gratitude to those around you, fostering a positive and supportive environment.

The practical tool encourages individuals to regularly express love and gratitude to those around them, fostering a positive and supportive environment. This approach emphasizes the power of positive interactions and the impact of expressing appreciation for the people in one's life.

Regularly Express Love and Gratitude:

1. Verbal Affirmations: Use verbal affirmations to express love and gratitude. Verbal expressions, such as saying "I love you" or "I appreciate you," have a profound impact on building positive connections and uplifting the spirits of those around you.

2. Written Notes and Messages: Write notes or send messages expressing love and gratitude. This could be in the form of handwritten letters, text messages, or emails. Written expressions provide a lasting reminder of your feelings and can be revisited by the recipients.

3. Acts of Kindness: Demonstrate love and gratitude through acts of kindness. Small gestures, such as helping with tasks, offering assistance, or surprising someone with a thoughtful gift, convey your appreciation for their presence in your life.

Foster a Positive and Supportive Environment:

1. Create a Culture of Positivity: Foster a culture of positivity in your relationships and environment. Regular expressions of love and gratitude contribute to a positive atmosphere where individuals feel valued and supported.

2. Acknowledge Achievements: Celebrate the achievements of others and acknowledge their contributions. Expressing gratitude for the efforts and accomplishments of those around you reinforces a sense of teamwork and mutual appreciation.

3. Encourage Open Communication: Create an environment where open communication is encouraged. Expressing love and

gratitude fosters trust and openness, making it easier for individuals to share their thoughts, feelings, and concerns.

How to Implement the Tool:

1. Daily Expressions: Make it a habit to express love and gratitude daily. This could involve expressing appreciation to family members, friends, colleagues, or anyone who plays a significant role in your life. Regularity enhances the positive impact.

2. Special Occasions: Seize special occasions, such as birthdays, anniversaries, or achievements, as opportunities to express love and gratitude in a more deliberate and focused manner. Use these moments to celebrate and appreciate the people you care about.

3. Random Acts of Kindness: Incorporate random acts of kindness into your routine. Surprise gestures, whether big or small, convey your love and gratitude unexpectedly, creating moments of joy and connection.

4. Gratitude Rituals: Establish gratitude rituals within your relationships. This could include sharing one thing you appreciate about each other before bedtime or having a regular gratitude session during family or team meetings.

5. Encourage Reciprocity: Encourage a culture of reciprocal expressions of love and gratitude. When others express their appreciation, respond in kind. This reciprocal exchange strengthens bonds and reinforces positive communication.

Benefits of Regularly Expressing Love and Gratitude:

1. Strengthened Relationships: Regular expressions of love and gratitude strengthen relationships by creating a foundation of

trust, appreciation, and mutual support. This contributes to healthier and more fulfilling connections.

2. Positive Emotional Well-Being: Both the giver and the recipient experience positive emotional well-being when love and gratitude are expressed. Acts of kindness and appreciation contribute to a sense of joy, fulfillment, and emotional warmth.

3. Improved Communication: Expressing love and gratitude fosters improved communication within relationships. It encourages open and honest dialogue, making it easier to navigate challenges and resolve conflicts in a constructive manner.

4. Enhanced Team Dynamics: In a team or group setting, expressing love and gratitude enhances team dynamics. Recognizing and appreciating the contributions of team members fosters a positive and collaborative work environment.

5. Cultivation of a Positive Culture: Regular expressions of love and gratitude contribute to the cultivation of a positive culture within families, friendships, and organizations. This positive culture becomes a source of resilience during challenging times.

Adapt to Your Preferences:

1. Tailor Expressions to Individuals: Tailor your expressions of love and gratitude to the preferences of individuals. Some may appreciate verbal affirmations, while others may find written notes more meaningful. Customize your approach to suit each person.

2. Explore Different Love Languages: Explore and understand the love languages of those around you. People may have different preferences in how they receive and express love. Whether it's

through words of affirmation, acts of service, gifts, quality time, or physical touch, adapt your expressions accordingly.

3. Rotate Focus: Rotate your focus among different individuals in your life. Ensure that expressions of love and gratitude are distributed among family members, friends, colleagues, and anyone else who plays a significant role.

4. Incorporate Rituals: Incorporate rituals into your expressions. Whether it's a weekly gratitude session or a monthly celebration of achievements, establishing rituals adds a sense of consistency and anticipation.

5. Encourage Peer-to-Peer Expressions: Encourage and facilitate expressions of love and gratitude among peers. Create an environment where individuals feel comfortable expressing appreciation for each other, fostering a culture of positivity within groups.

By regularly expressing love and gratitude, individuals contribute to the creation of positive and supportive environments. This tool is a powerful way to nurture meaningful connections, strengthen relationships, and cultivate a culture of appreciation within personal and professional spheres.

67) Let Your Actions Speak Louder Than Your Words:

Anecdote: Imagine a mentor leading by example. Actions have a lasting impact beyond words.

Interpretation: Demonstrate your values through your behavior.

Practical Tool: Align your actions with your principles, understanding that actions convey your true beliefs.

The practical tool emphasizes the importance of aligning your actions with your principles, recognizing that actions serve as a reflection of your true beliefs. This approach underscores the significance of integrity and authenticity in one's behavior.

Align Your Actions with Your Principles:

1. Clarify Your Principles: Begin by clarifying your principles and core beliefs. Identify the values and ethical guidelines that are fundamental to your identity. These principles serve as the foundation for aligning your actions with your authentic self.

2. Integrity in Decision-Making: Practice integrity in decision-making. When faced with choices, consider whether each option aligns with your principles. Make decisions that resonate with your values, even when it requires courage or goes against the norm.

3. Consistency in Behavior: Strive for consistency in your behavior. Aligning actions with principles involves maintaining a coherent and uniform approach to situations. Consistency builds trust and authenticity in your interactions with others.

Understanding Actions as Belief Conveyors:

1. Authenticity in Expression: Recognize that actions are powerful conveyors of beliefs. Authenticity in expressing your principles through actions reinforces the sincerity of your convictions. Others can perceive and trust your authenticity when actions align with stated beliefs.

2. Behavior as Communication: View your behavior as a form of communication. It communicates your true beliefs and values to

others, often more effectively than words alone. Be mindful of the messages your actions convey to ensure they align with your principles.

3. Impact on Relationships: Understand the impact of aligned actions on relationships. Consistently demonstrating your principles through actions fosters trust and credibility. Others are more likely to respect and connect with you when they perceive a genuine alignment between your words and deeds.

How to Implement the Tool:

1. Reflect on Principles: Regularly reflect on your principles and values. Consider what matters most to you and how your beliefs guide your choices. This self-reflection is essential for maintaining clarity about your principles.

2. Evaluate Potential Actions: Before taking any significant action, evaluate it in the context of your principles. Ask yourself whether the action aligns with your values and ethical standards. This intentional assessment ensures that your decisions are in harmony with your beliefs.

3. Seek Feedback: Seek feedback from trusted individuals. Share your principles with those close to you and invite honest feedback on how well your actions align with your stated beliefs. External perspectives can provide valuable insights.

4. Course Correction: Be open to course correction. If you recognize misalignments between your actions and principles, be willing to make adjustments. Acknowledge areas where improvement is needed and take proactive steps to realign your behavior.

5. Hold Yourself Accountable: Establish a system of accountability for yourself. Whether through self-reflection, journaling, or regular check-ins, hold yourself accountable for maintaining alignment between your principles and actions.

Benefits of Aligning Actions with Principles:

1. Integrity and Trust: Alignment between actions and principles builds a reputation for integrity. Others are more likely to trust and respect individuals who consistently demonstrate their values through their actions.

2. Authenticity and Credibility: Authenticity in action enhances credibility. Individuals who authentically live by their principles are perceived as genuine and reliable, reinforcing their credibility in personal and professional relationships.

3. Stronger Character Development: Consistent alignment between principles and actions contributes to stronger character development. It fosters self-awareness, personal growth, and a deep understanding of one's values.

4. Positive Impact on Environment: Individuals who align actions with principles contribute to positive environments. Whether in a family, workplace, or community, their influence helps create cultures that reflect shared values and ethical standards.

5. Enhanced Decision-Making: A clear alignment with principles simplifies decision-making. When facing choices, individuals who prioritize principles can more easily discern which options resonate with their beliefs, leading to more confident and ethical decisions.

Adapt to Your Preferences:

1. Personalize Your Principles: Personalize your principles based on your unique values and beliefs. Your principles are a reflection of your individuality, and tailoring them to resonate with your personal convictions enhances the authenticity of your actions.

2. Create Action Plans: Create action plans that reflect your principles. Identify specific actions that demonstrate your commitment to each principle. This proactive approach helps translate abstract values into tangible behaviors.

3. Flexible Application: Recognize that the application of principles may require flexibility in different contexts. While the core values remain consistent, the specific actions taken may vary based on the nuances of each situation.

4. Solicit Diverse Perspectives: Solicit diverse perspectives to enrich your understanding of principles. Engage in conversations with individuals who may have different perspectives, allowing you to refine and broaden your principles through thoughtful dialogue.

5. Continuous Refinement: View the alignment of actions and principles as a continuous process of refinement. As you grow and evolve, your principles may undergo adjustments. Embrace the opportunity for continuous improvement and adaptation.

By aligning actions with principles, individuals contribute to a more authentic and ethical world. This tool serves as a guide for navigating decisions, fostering trust, and building meaningful connections with others based on shared values and beliefs.

68) Value Inner Wealth Over External Validation:

Anecdote: Picture a well of self-worth. It's filled by internal accomplishments, not external praise.

Interpretation: Rely on your internal compass for validation rather than seeking it externally.

Practical Tool: Reflect on your values and achievements as sources of self-worth, rather than relying solely on others' opinions.

The practical tool encourages individuals to derive their self-worth from reflecting on their values and achievements rather than relying solely on others' opinions. This approach emphasizes the importance of internal validation and self-awareness in building a positive sense of self.

Reflect on Your Values and Achievements:

1. Clarify Your Values: Begin by clarifying your core values. Identify the principles and beliefs that are important to you and contribute to your sense of identity. This clarity provides a foundation for assessing your actions and decisions.

2. Recognize Personal Achievements: Acknowledge and recognize your personal achievements. These achievements can be both big and small, encompassing various aspects of your life such as career accomplishments, personal growth, or overcoming challenges. Reflect on the skills and strengths that have contributed to your successes.

3. Internal Validation: Shift the focus from external validation to internal validation. Instead of relying solely on others' opinions for validation, cultivate a sense of self-worth by recognizing and appreciating your values, achievements, and the positive qualities you bring to different aspects of your life.

Why Self-Worth from Values and Achievements Matters:

1. Stability in Self-Esteem: Deriving self-worth from values and achievements provides a more stable foundation for self-esteem. External opinions can fluctuate, but the acknowledgment of your intrinsic worth and accomplishments offers a consistent source of confidence.

2. Empowerment and Autonomy: Embracing self-worth based on values and achievements empowers you to take ownership of your identity. It fosters autonomy and the ability to make decisions aligned with your values rather than seeking constant approval from others.

3. Resilience in the Face of Criticism: When self-worth is rooted in values and achievements, individuals are better equipped to navigate criticism. The ability to reflect on personal accomplishments and adherence to core values provides resilience against external judgments.

4. Internal Fulfillment: Internal fulfillment is often more sustainable than relying on external validation. Reflecting on your values and achievements allows you to find intrinsic meaning and satisfaction in your actions, contributing to a sense of fulfillment.

How to Implement the Tool:

1. Regular Values Assessment: Conduct regular assessments of your values. Reflect on whether your actions align with your core values and whether you are living in accordance with the principles that matter most to you. This self-awareness reinforces a sense of integrity.

2. Celebrate Personal Milestones: Celebrate your personal milestones. Whether it's completing a project, achieving a personal goal, or overcoming a challenge, take time to acknowledge and celebrate your achievements. This positive reinforcement contributes to a healthy self-view.

3. Create a Values Statement: Develop a values statement that encapsulates your core beliefs and principles. This concise statement can serve as a reminder of what is truly important to you and guide your decision-making.

4. Practice Self-Reflection: Engage in regular self-reflection. Take moments to pause and contemplate your values, actions, and achievements. Consider how these aspects contribute to your overall sense of self-worth.

5. Set Intrinsic Goals: Set goals that are intrinsically motivated. Instead of pursuing goals solely for external recognition, consider what aligns with your values and personal growth. Achieving goals that resonate with your values reinforces your sense of accomplishment.

Benefits of Reflecting on Values and Achievements:

1. Increased Self-Understanding: Regular reflection on values and achievements fosters increased self-understanding. Understanding your values allows you to make choices that align with your authentic self, contributing to a more genuine sense of identity.

2. Greater Confidence: Deriving self-worth from values and achievements enhances confidence. Recognizing your abilities and accomplishments provides a strong foundation for navigating challenges and pursuing new endeavors with belief in your capabilities.

3. Enhanced Decision-Making: A clear understanding of your values serves as a guide for decision-making. Reflecting on your values before making choices ensures that your actions are in harmony with what truly matters to you.

4. Cultivation of Intrinsic Motivation: Reflecting on achievements rooted in values cultivates intrinsic motivation. Intrinsic motivation, driven by personal satisfaction and alignment with values, is a powerful force for ongoing growth and achievement.

5. Resilience in the Face of External Pressures: When self-worth is derived from values and achievements, individuals are more resilient in the face of external pressures and societal expectations. The ability to reflect on personal accomplishments provides a sense of purpose that withstands external scrutiny.

Adapt to Your Preferences:

1. Create a Personal Ritual: Establish a personal ritual for reflection. This could be a daily practice of journaling, a weekly review of achievements, or a monthly values assessment. Tailor the frequency and format to suit your preferences.

2. Incorporate Values in Goal-Setting: Incorporate your values into goal-setting. When setting goals, consider how they align with your core values. This approach ensures that your pursuits are meaningful and contribute to your overall well-being.

3. Seek Feedback Aligned with Values: When seeking feedback, prioritize input that aligns with your values. Evaluate feedback in the context of your principles and choose to integrate insights that resonate with your authentic self.

4. Share Achievements with Trusted Individuals: Share your achievements with trusted individuals who understand and appreciate your values. Celebrating successes with those who share your values enhances the positive impact of these moments.

5. Adjust Based on Personal Growth: Be open to adjusting your values and reflections based on personal growth. As you evolve, your values may also shift. Embrace this evolution and adapt your reflections accordingly.

By reflecting on values and achievements as sources of self-worth, individuals cultivate a deeper understanding of themselves, fostering confidence, resilience, and a sense of purpose. This tool empowers individuals to prioritize internal validation, contributing to a more authentic and fulfilling life.

69) Foster a Growth Mindset:

Anecdote: Imagine a garden of potential. A growth mindset sees challenges as opportunities to bloom.

Interpretation: Embrace challenges as chances to learn and improve.

Practical Tool: Approach difficulties with curiosity, viewing them as stepping stones toward personal development.

The practical tool encourages individuals to approach difficulties with curiosity, viewing them as stepping stones toward personal development. This approach promotes a mindset shift where challenges are seen as opportunities for growth and learning.

Approach Difficulties with Curiosity:

1. Curiosity as a Mindset: Cultivate curiosity as a mindset when facing difficulties. Instead of approaching challenges with resistance or frustration, adopt a curious attitude. This involves asking questions, seeking understanding, and maintaining an open and inquisitive outlook.

2. Viewing Challenges as Opportunities: Shift your perspective to view difficulties as opportunities for personal development. Recognize that each challenge presents a chance to learn, adapt, and grow. Embrace the idea that overcoming obstacles contributes to your overall progress.

3. Learning Orientation: Develop a learning orientation in the face of difficulties. Focus on acquiring new skills, gaining insights,

and expanding your knowledge during challenging situations. This proactive approach transforms challenges into valuable learning experiences.

Why Curiosity and Personal Development Matter:

1. Resilience Building: Approaching difficulties with curiosity builds resilience. Instead of being deterred by setbacks, a curious mindset allows you to bounce back more effectively by seeking solutions and adapting to changing circumstances.

2. Continuous Learning: Embracing challenges as opportunities for personal development promotes continuous learning. Curiosity fuels a desire to understand, improve, and acquire new knowledge and skills, fostering a mindset of lifelong learning.

3. Adaptability in Change: Difficulties often accompany change, and a curious mindset enhances adaptability. When faced with changes or uncertainties, viewing them with curiosity enables you to navigate transitions more smoothly and find creative solutions.

4. Enhanced Problem-Solving: Curiosity contributes to enhanced problem-solving skills. Instead of being overwhelmed by difficulties, a curious approach encourages you to analyze situations, explore alternative perspectives, and generate innovative solutions.

How to Implement the Tool:

1. Ask Questions: When confronted with difficulties, ask questions to better understand the situation. Inquire about the root causes, potential solutions, and the lessons that can be extracted. Curiosity stimulates a deeper exploration of challenges.

2. Seek Different Perspectives: Expand your viewpoint by seeking different perspectives. Engage in conversations with others who may offer unique insights or experiences related to the difficulty at hand. Embrace diversity in thought and approach.

3. Experiment with Solutions: Approach difficulties as opportunities to experiment with solutions. Rather than being fixed on one approach, be open to trying different strategies. Curiosity encourages experimentation and the discovery of effective methods.

4. Celebrate Small Wins: Acknowledge and celebrate small wins along the way. Recognize the progress you make during the process of overcoming difficulties. Each small achievement contributes to your personal development journey.

5. Document Lessons Learned: Keep a record of lessons learned from each difficulty. Whether through journaling or note-taking, document the insights, skills acquired, and personal growth experienced during challenging times. This reflection reinforces the positive impact of curiosity.

Benefits of Approaching Difficulties with Curiosity:

1. Positive Mindset: A curious approach to difficulties fosters a positive mindset. Instead of seeing challenges as roadblocks, curiosity reframes them as opportunities for exploration and improvement, contributing to overall well-being.

2. Increased Motivation: Curiosity is a powerful motivator. The desire to understand, learn, and grow fuels intrinsic motivation. Approaching difficulties with curiosity enhances your drive to overcome obstacles and achieve meaningful outcomes.

3. Emotional Resilience: Curiosity contributes to emotional resilience. When faced with setbacks, a curious mindset helps regulate emotions and maintain composure. This emotional resilience is essential for navigating challenges effectively.
4. Continuous Personal Development: Difficulties become a catalyst for continuous personal development. Curiosity propels you to seek opportunities for growth in various aspects of your life, ensuring that challenges contribute positively to your overall development.
5. Adoption of a Growth Mindset: Embracing difficulties with curiosity aligns with the principles of a growth mindset. Instead of viewing abilities as fixed, a growth mindset sees challenges as opportunities to develop and refine skills over time.

Adapt to Your Preferences:

1. Customize Curiosity Practices: Customize your curiosity practices based on what works for you. This could include regular reflection, seeking mentorship, attending workshops, or engaging in self-directed learning. Tailor your approach to align with your preferences.
2. Incorporate Curiosity in Daily Life: Make curiosity a part of your daily life. Whether it's exploring new topics, trying out different activities, or engaging in conversations with diverse individuals, find ways to infuse curiosity into your routine.
3. Establish Curiosity Rituals: Establish rituals that encourage curiosity. This could involve setting aside time each week for exploration, dedicating a curiosity journal, or participating in activities that stimulate your inquisitive nature.

4. Balance Reflection and Action: Strike a balance between reflection and action. While reflection fuels curiosity, taking proactive steps to address difficulties ensures that you translate your curiosity into tangible personal development.

5. Adapt Curiosity to Various Contexts: Recognize that curiosity can be adapted to various contexts. Whether you're facing challenges in your professional life, personal relationships, or self-discovery, apply curiosity as a universal tool for growth.

Approaching difficulties with curiosity transforms them from obstacles to opportunities. This tool empowers individuals to embrace challenges as integral parts of their personal development journey, fostering resilience, motivation, and a continuous pursuit of growth.

70) Practice Random Acts of Kindness:

Anecdote: Picture a ripple effect of goodwill. Small acts of kindness create a positive impact.

Interpretation: Spread positivity through unexpected gestures of kindness.

Practical Tool: Incorporate random acts of kindness into your daily life, contributing to a culture of compassion.

The practical tool encourages individuals to incorporate random acts of kindness into their daily lives, contributing to a culture of compassion. This approach promotes the idea that small, unexpected gestures of kindness can have a significant positive impact on individuals and society as a whole.

Incorporate Random Acts of Kindness:

1. Define Random Acts of Kindness: Random acts of kindness refer to spontaneous, unplanned gestures of goodwill toward others. These acts can range from simple, everyday kindness to more significant efforts, all with the intention of bringing positivity and compassion to those around you.

2. Make Kindness a Habit: Integrate kindness into your daily routine until it becomes a habit. Consistently looking for opportunities to perform acts of kindness reinforces a mindset of compassion and empathy. Small gestures, when repeated, contribute to a positive and uplifting environment.

3. Diverse Acts of Kindness: Embrace a variety of kindness actions. Acts of kindness can be as simple as offering a genuine compliment, holding the door for someone, or actively listening to a friend. Additionally, consider more intentional acts such as volunteering or supporting charitable causes.

Why Random Acts of Kindness Matter:

1. Positive Ripple Effect: Random acts of kindness create a positive ripple effect. When you extend kindness to others, it often inspires a chain reaction, as recipients may be motivated to pay it forward, fostering a culture of compassion and generosity.

2. Enhanced Well-Being: Engaging in acts of kindness has been linked to enhanced well-being. Both the giver and the recipient experience positive emotions, contributing to a sense of joy, gratitude, and overall life satisfaction.

3. Strengthens Social Connections: Acts of kindness strengthen social connections. Whether it's within your family, workplace, or community, kindness fosters a sense of unity and camaraderie. Shared positive experiences contribute to stronger and more supportive relationships.
4. Cultivates Empathy: Regularly practicing random acts of kindness cultivates empathy. By considering the needs and feelings of others, individuals become more attuned to the experiences of those around them, fostering a deeper understanding and connection.

How to Implement the Tool:

1. Start Small: Begin with small acts of kindness. Smile at strangers, offer assistance, or express appreciation. Starting small allows you to build the habit gradually and encourages a consistent practice.
2. Be Observant: Pay attention to your surroundings and the people you encounter. Being observant enables you to identify opportunities for kindness that may arise unexpectedly. Look for ways to brighten someone's day in both ordinary and extraordinary situations.
3. Customize Acts of Kindness: Customize acts of kindness based on the preferences and needs of those around you. Tailoring your gestures ensures that they are meaningful and resonate with the individuals you are aiming to impact.
4. Keep it Genuine: Authenticity is key. Ensure that your acts of kindness are genuine and come from a sincere desire to

contribute positively to someone's day. Authentic kindness is more likely to be well-received and appreciated.

5. Encourage Others: Encourage others to join in. Share your experiences with random acts of kindness and inspire those around you to incorporate similar practices into their lives. Collective efforts contribute to a culture of compassion within communities.

Benefits of Incorporating Random Acts of Kindness:

1. Uplifts Mood and Well-Being: Engaging in acts of kindness has a direct positive impact on mood and well-being. The sense of fulfillment and joy derived from spreading kindness contributes to overall emotional and mental wellness.

2. Strengthens Community Bonds: Random acts of kindness strengthen bonds within communities. Shared positive experiences create a sense of unity and connectedness, fostering a supportive and caring environment.

3. Promotes a Culture of Compassion: Consistent acts of kindness contribute to the promotion of a culture of compassion. Over time, these actions become embedded in the social fabric, influencing the way people interact and care for one another.

4. Encourages Positive Behavior: Acts of kindness encourage positive behavior. When individuals experience kindness, they are more likely to reciprocate and engage in positive actions themselves, perpetuating a cycle of goodwill.

5. Contributes to Personal Growth: Engaging in acts of kindness contributes to personal growth. It provides opportunities to

develop empathy, generosity, and a broader perspective on the impact of one's actions, fostering continuous self-improvement.

Adapt to Your Preferences:

1. Select Acts Based on Strengths: Choose acts of kindness that align with your strengths and preferences. Whether it's offering your time, sharing a skill, or providing emotional support, selecting actions that resonate with you enhances the authenticity of your kindness.

2. Vary the Frequency: Vary the frequency of your kindness practices based on your schedule and preferences. You can engage in daily acts, weekly initiatives, or participate in occasional larger-scale kindness projects. Adapt the frequency to suit your lifestyle.

3. Involve Others in Planning: Involve others in planning acts of kindness. Collaborating with friends, family, or colleagues to organize kindness initiatives enhances the collective impact and fosters a sense of shared purpose.

4. Document Your Experiences: Keep a record of your experiences with acts of kindness. Documenting your actions, the reactions of others, and the overall impact provides a tangible reflection of the positive influence you're contributing to the world.

5. Integrate into Daily Routine: Integrate acts of kindness into your daily routine. Whether it's part of your morning ritual, during work hours, or as you wind down in the evening, incorporating kindness into your regular activities ensures its seamless integration into your lifestyle.

Incorporating random acts of kindness into daily life is a powerful tool for fostering a culture of compassion. It elevates individual well-being, strengthens community bonds, and contributes to the creation of a more caring and empathetic world.

71) Celebrate Others' Success Without Envy:

Anecdote: Picture a shared victory. Celebrating others' success creates a harmonious atmosphere.

Interpretation: Support and uplift others in their achievements without comparing or feeling envious.

Practical Tool: Cultivate a mindset that recognizes the success of others as inspiration rather than competition.

The practical tool encourages individuals to cultivate a mindset that recognizes the success of others as inspiration rather than competition. This approach promotes a positive and collaborative perspective, where the achievements of others are viewed as sources of motivation and learning rather than threats.

Cultivate a Mindset of Collaboration and Inspiration:

1. Shift from Competition to Collaboration: Embrace a mindset shift from seeing others as competitors to viewing them as collaborators. Recognize that success is not a limited resource and that the achievements of others can contribute to collective growth.

2. Acknowledge Diverse Paths to Success: Understand that there are diverse paths to success. Each individual's journey is unique, and success can be achieved through different routes.

Acknowledging this diversity allows you to appreciate the richness of experiences and learning opportunities.

3. Celebrate Others' Achievements: Celebrate the successes of others genuinely. Instead of feeling threatened or envious, cultivate a spirit of joy and enthusiasm when witnessing the accomplishments of your peers. Celebrating others' achievements creates a positive and supportive environment.

Why Recognizing Others' Success Matters:

1. Promotes a Positive Work Environment: Recognizing and celebrating the success of others contributes to a positive work or social environment. A culture that values collaboration over competition fosters a sense of camaraderie and mutual support.

2. Inspires Motivation and Resilience: Viewing others' success as inspiration can be a powerful motivator. Instead of demoralizing you, the achievements of others can inspire you to set higher goals, work harder, and develop resilience in pursuing your own objectives.

3. Encourages Continuous Learning: Recognizing others' success encourages a mindset of continuous learning. By studying the strategies and approaches that led to their achievements, you can gain valuable insights and apply them to your own endeavors.

4. Strengthens Professional and Personal Relationships: A mindset of recognizing others' success fosters strong professional and personal relationships. Collaborating with individuals who share their experiences and insights enhances your network and creates opportunities for mutual growth.

How to Implement the Tool:

1. Practice Genuine Empathy: Cultivate genuine empathy toward others. Understand the effort, dedication, and challenges individuals may have faced on their journey to success. This understanding fosters a supportive mindset rather than one rooted in competition.

2. Seek Mentorship and Guidance: Engage with successful individuals as mentors or sources of guidance. Rather than perceiving them as rivals, approach them for mentorship. Many successful individuals are open to sharing their experiences and providing valuable advice.

3. Focus on Personal Growth: Shift your focus from external competition to personal growth. Set goals that align with your values and aspirations, emphasizing your own development rather than comparing yourself to others.

4. Express Sincere Congratulations: When someone achieves success, express sincere congratulations. Whether through verbal acknowledgment, a congratulatory message, or a thoughtful gesture, showing genuine support contributes to a positive and collaborative atmosphere.

5. Participate in Collaborative Initiatives: Engage in collaborative initiatives. Rather than competing for individual recognition, join efforts that contribute to shared success. Collaborative projects allow you to leverage collective strengths and celebrate achievements together.

Benefits of Cultivating an Inspirational Mindset:

1. Positive Workplace or Social Culture: An inspirational mindset contributes to a positive workplace or social culture. Instead of fostering a competitive atmosphere, it promotes a supportive environment where individuals uplift each other.

2. Increased Motivation and Productivity: Recognizing others' success as inspiration enhances motivation and productivity. It transforms the energy spent on comparison and competition into a driving force for personal improvement and achievement.

3. Builds Stronger Relationships: Building a mindset of inspiration builds stronger relationships. Colleagues, friends, and peers are more likely to collaborate and support each other when success is viewed as a collective endeavor.

4. Encourages Innovation: Collaboration and inspiration often lead to innovation. When individuals share insights and ideas, the collective creativity and problem-solving capacity increase, fostering an environment where innovation thrives.

5. Promotes a Growth Mindset: Embracing others' success as inspiration aligns with a growth mindset. Instead of viewing abilities as fixed, this mindset sees challenges and success as opportunities for continuous learning and improvement.

Adapt to Your Preferences:

1. Reflect on Personal Growth: Regularly reflect on your personal growth. Assess your achievements, challenges, and areas for improvement without comparing yourself to others. This reflective practice reinforces an intrinsic focus on your journey.

2. Join Collaborative Communities: Join communities or networks that emphasize collaboration and shared success. Being part of such groups provides a supportive environment where members celebrate each other's achievements and offer valuable insights.
3. Set Collective Goals: Set goals that involve collective success. Whether within a team or a broader community, align your objectives with shared goals that contribute to the success of the group.
4. Encourage a Positive Mindset in Others: Encourage a positive and inspirational mindset in others. Foster a culture where individuals support each other, recognize achievements, and contribute to a shared atmosphere of growth and success.
5. Celebrate Milestones Together: Celebrate milestones together. Whether in the workplace or personal life, create opportunities to acknowledge and celebrate collective achievements. This shared celebration reinforces a collaborative mindset.

Cultivating a mindset that recognizes the success of others as inspiration rather than competition is a transformative tool that contributes to a positive, collaborative, and growth-oriented environment. It empowers individuals to find motivation in the achievements of their peers, fostering a culture of support and shared success.

72) Celebrate Others' Success Without Envy:

Anecdote: Imagine a library with endless volumes. Lifelong learning is a journey of perpetual growth.

Interpretation: Keep your mind open to new ideas, fostering a love for learning throughout life.

Practical Tool: Dedicate time to explore new subjects, acquire new skills, and stay intellectually curious.

The practical tool encourages individuals to dedicate time to explore new subjects, acquire new skills, and stay intellectually curious. This approach emphasizes the importance of continuous learning, curiosity, and personal growth.

Dedicate Time to Intellectual Exploration:

1. Allocate Time for Learning: Set aside dedicated time in your schedule for intellectual exploration. Whether it's a specific time each day, a few hours per week, or regular intervals, allocating time demonstrates a commitment to continuous learning.

2. Choose Diverse Subjects: Explore a diverse range of subjects. Choose topics that intrigue you, challenge your existing knowledge, or align with your personal interests. Diversifying your exploration broadens your perspective and enriches your understanding of the world.

3. Engage in Active Learning: Adopt active learning methods. Rather than passively consuming information, engage in activities that reinforce understanding. This could include discussions, practical applications, or teaching concepts to others, enhancing retention and application.

Why Intellectual Exploration Matters:

1. Fosters Lifelong Learning: Intellectual exploration fosters a mindset of lifelong learning. Embracing the idea that learning is a continuous process encourages a proactive approach to acquiring new knowledge and skills throughout life.

2. Stimulates Curiosity and Creativity: Regular exploration stimulates curiosity and creativity. Engaging with new subjects and ideas prompts innovative thinking, problem-solving, and the ability to connect seemingly unrelated concepts.

3. Adapts to Changing Environments: In a rapidly changing world, intellectual exploration helps individuals adapt to evolving environments. Acquiring diverse skills and knowledge enhances adaptability, ensuring you can navigate different situations effectively.

4. Enhances Cognitive Abilities: Continuous learning contributes to enhanced cognitive abilities. Keeping the brain active through intellectual exploration promotes mental agility, memory retention, and critical thinking skills.

How to Implement the Tool:

1. Create a Learning Plan: Develop a learning plan that outlines the subjects or skills you want to explore. This plan could include short-term and long-term goals, milestones, and specific activities to achieve them.

2. Utilize Various Learning Resources: Take advantage of a variety of learning resources. This includes books, online courses, podcasts, workshops, mentorship, and hands-on experiences.

Diversifying your sources ensures a well-rounded and comprehensive learning experience.

3. Document Your Learning Journey: Keep a journal or documentation of your learning journey. Record insights, discoveries, challenges, and how new knowledge or skills are applied in your life. Reflecting on your progress reinforces the value of continuous exploration.

4. Engage in Discussions and Communities: Participate in discussions and communities related to your areas of interest. Engaging with others who share similar passions provides opportunities for knowledge exchange, collaboration, and exposure to different perspectives.

5. Set Challenging Goals: Set challenging but achievable learning goals. Strive to explore subjects or acquire skills that stretch your current capabilities. Setting challenging goals stimulates growth and keeps intellectual exploration exciting.

Benefits of Intellectual Exploration:

1. Personal Growth and Development: Intellectual exploration contributes to personal growth and development. Acquiring new knowledge and skills enhances your capabilities, confidence, and overall well-being.

2. Increased Adaptability: Continuous learning improves adaptability. The ability to quickly acquire and apply new information ensures you can navigate diverse situations and thrive in changing environments.

3. Stimulates Innovation: Intellectual exploration stimulates innovation. Exposure to diverse ideas and perspectives sparks

creative thinking, leading to innovative solutions and approaches to challenges.

4. Expands Knowledge Base: Regular exploration expands your knowledge base. A broader understanding of various subjects enables you to make informed decisions, contribute meaningfully to discussions, and connect ideas across different domains.

5. Enhanced Problem-Solving Skills: Active engagement in intellectual exploration hones problem-solving skills. Tackling new subjects and challenges strengthens your ability to analyze, strategize, and find effective solutions to complex problems.

Adapt to Your Preferences:

1. Tailor Learning Methods: Tailor your learning methods to suit your preferences. Whether you prefer reading, hands-on experiences, visual learning, or interactive discussions, adapt your approach to maximize engagement and retention.

2. Blend Learning with Daily Routine: Integrate intellectual exploration into your daily routine. Whether it's dedicating time in the morning, during breaks, or before bedtime, blending learning with your routine ensures consistency and sustainable habits.

3. Collaborate with Learning Partners: Collaborate with learning partners or study groups. Sharing the exploration journey with others provides motivation, accountability, and opportunities for collaborative learning experiences.

4. Explore Interdisciplinary Connections: Explore interdisciplinary connections between subjects. Identify overlaps and connections between seemingly unrelated areas of interest. This

interdisciplinary approach enriches your understanding and promotes holistic learning.

5. Celebrate Learning Milestones: Celebrate milestones in your learning journey. Recognize and celebrate achievements, whether they are completing a course, mastering a new skill, or gaining insights that contribute to your personal and professional growth.

Dedicating time to explore new subjects, acquire new skills, and stay intellectually curious is a transformative tool that empowers individuals to embrace a lifelong learning mindset. It opens doors to personal growth, innovation, and adaptability, fostering a proactive approach to continuous intellectual exploration.

73) Balance Rest and Productivity:

Anecdote: Picture a well-maintained garden. Rest is as crucial as growth for sustained productivity.

Interpretation: Prioritize rest to recharge and maintain long-term productivity.

Practical Tool: Establish a healthy balance between work and rest, recognizing the importance of both for overall well-being.

The practical tool encourages individuals to establish a healthy balance between work and rest, recognizing the importance of both for overall well-being. This approach emphasizes the significance of maintaining equilibrium in one's professional and personal life to promote mental, physical, and emotional health.

Establish a Healthy Work-Rest Balance:

1. Define Boundaries: Clearly define boundaries between work and rest. Set specific working hours and stick to them, creating a

clear separation between professional responsibilities and personal time. Establishing boundaries helps prevent work from encroaching into periods dedicated to rest and relaxation.

2. Prioritize Self-Care: Prioritize self-care as an integral part of your routine. Allocate time for activities that contribute to your well-being, such as exercise, mindfulness practices, hobbies, and quality time with loved ones. Recognize self-care as essential for maintaining balance and resilience.

3. Set Realistic Work Goals: Set realistic and achievable work goals. Establishing clear objectives helps manage workload and prevents the accumulation of excessive tasks, reducing stress and creating a healthier work environment.

4. Take Regular Breaks: Incorporate regular breaks into your workday. Short breaks enhance focus, creativity, and overall productivity. Whether it's a brief walk, stretching exercises, or a few moments of relaxation, breaks contribute to sustained energy levels.

Why Work-Rest Balance Matters:

1. Preserves Mental and Emotional Well-Being: Maintaining a healthy work-rest balance preserves mental and emotional well-being. Avoiding prolonged periods of stress and burnout is crucial for mental clarity, emotional resilience, and the prevention of mental health challenges.

2. Enhances Physical Health: Striking a balance between work and rest supports physical health. Adequate rest, sleep, and relaxation contribute to improved immune function, increased energy

levels, and reduced risk of physical health issues associated with chronic stress.

3. Promotes Sustainable Productivity: A balanced approach promotes sustainable productivity. Rested individuals are more likely to perform effectively, make sound decisions, and sustain long-term professional success. Avoiding overwork fosters a more sustainable and fulfilling career.

4. Strengthens Relationships: Balancing work and rest strengthens relationships. Quality time spent with family and friends contributes to social connections, emotional support, and overall life satisfaction. Nurturing relationships outside of work is vital for holistic well-being.

How to Implement the Tool:

1. Establish a Routine: Develop a consistent daily or weekly routine that incorporates both work and rest. A structured routine provides a framework for managing responsibilities while ensuring dedicated time for relaxation and personal activities.

2. Communicate Boundaries: Communicate your boundaries to colleagues, friends, and family. Clearly express your working hours and when you'll be available for personal time. Effective communication helps manage expectations and prevents undue pressure to extend work hours.

3. Prioritize Tasks: Prioritize tasks based on urgency and importance. This allows you to focus on critical work during designated hours while ensuring non-urgent tasks do not interfere with planned periods of rest. Prioritization supports a more balanced workload.

4. Learn to Say No: Develop the ability to say no when necessary. Recognize your limits and avoid overcommitting to tasks or responsibilities that could disrupt your work-rest balance. Setting healthy boundaries requires the occasional refusal of additional commitments.

Benefits of Work-Rest Balance:

1. Improved Mental Resilience: Maintaining a healthy balance enhances mental resilience. Adequate rest and relaxation contribute to stress reduction, preventing mental exhaustion and promoting mental clarity.

2. Enhanced Productivity and Creativity: A balanced approach enhances productivity and creativity. Well-rested individuals are more likely to approach tasks with focus, creativity, and a fresh perspective, leading to improved problem-solving and innovation.

3. Better Physical Health: Striking a balance between work and rest supports better physical health. Regular rest contributes to improved immune function, reduced risk of chronic illnesses, and overall physical well-being.

4. Positive Impact on Relationships: Balancing work and rest positively impacts relationships. Quality time spent with loved ones strengthens emotional connections and contributes to a supportive social network, enhancing overall life satisfaction.

Adapt to Your Preferences:

1. Flexible Work Hours: f possible, negotiate flexible work hours that align with your peak productivity and well-being. Flexibility

allows you to customize your work schedule to better suit your preferences and balance.

2. Experiment with Work-Rest Patterns: Experiment with different work-rest patterns to find what works best for you. Whether it's alternating focused work sessions with short breaks or implementing a specific rest day each week, adapt the approach to your preferences and needs.

3. Regularly Assess and Adjust: Regularly assess your work-rest balance and adjust as needed. Life circumstances, workloads, and personal priorities may change, requiring periodic evaluations and adjustments to maintain equilibrium.

4. Involve Others in Planning: Involve others in planning your work-rest balance. Collaborate with family members, friends, or colleagues to create a supportive environment that respects your boundaries and encourages a healthy approach to both work and rest.

Establishing a healthy balance between work and rest is a transformative tool that contributes to overall well-being. It promotes sustained professional success, enhances physical and mental health, and strengthens personal relationships. Prioritizing this balance ensures a fulfilling and sustainable approach to both professional and personal aspects of life.

74) Cultivate a Sense of Wonder:

Anecdote: Imagine a child exploring the world. Cultivating wonder keeps life vibrant and full of discovery.

Interpretation: Approach life with curiosity and awe, maintaining a youthful sense of wonder.

Practical Tool: Regularly engage in activities that evoke a sense of wonder, fostering appreciation for the world around you.

The practical tool encourages individuals to regularly engage in activities that evoke a sense of wonder, fostering appreciation for the world around them. This approach emphasizes the importance of cultivating a curious and appreciative mindset by actively seeking awe-inspiring experiences.

Regularly Engage in Wonder-Inducing Activities:

1. Nature Exploration: Spend time in nature to witness its beauty and grandeur. Whether it's a walk in the park, a hike in the mountains, or a visit to the beach, immersing yourself in natural surroundings can evoke a sense of wonder and appreciation for the Earth's wonders.

2. Stargazing: Set aside time for stargazing. Observing the night sky, identifying constellations, and marveling at the vastness of the universe can evoke a profound sense of wonder and awe.

3. Art and Culture: Explore art galleries, museums, or cultural events. Engaging with various forms of art, whether visual arts, music, or performances, can evoke emotions and inspire a deep appreciation for human creativity.

4. Scientific Exploration: Dive into scientific discoveries and exploration. Whether through documentaries, educational programs, or hands-on experiments, delving into the wonders of science can spark a sense of awe and curiosity.

Why Eliciting Wonder Matters:

1. Enhances Well-Being: Experiencing wonder has been linked to enhanced well-being. It can elevate mood, reduce stress, and contribute to an overall sense of happiness and fulfillment.

2. Fosters Curiosity: Wonder fosters curiosity. When individuals encounter awe-inspiring moments, they are often prompted to seek a deeper understanding, asking questions and exploring the intricacies of what they've experienced.

3. Promotes Gratitude: Experiencing wonder promotes gratitude. Acknowledging the beauty and marvels of the world fosters a sense of thankfulness and appreciation for the aspects of life that might be taken for granted.

4. Expands Perspectives: Wonder expands perspectives. It encourages individuals to see beyond their immediate surroundings and consider the broader context of existence, fostering a more open-minded and inclusive worldview.

How to Implement the Tool:

1. Create Wonder Journals: Keep a wonder journal where you record moments that evoke a sense of wonder. Describe the experiences, emotions, and thoughts associated with these moments. Regularly revisit your journal to reflect on and appreciate these wonders.

2. Plan Wonder-Inducing Adventures: Actively plan and participate in wonder-inducing adventures. Whether it's exploring a new place, attending cultural events, or trying new activities, intentionally seek out experiences that evoke awe and amazement.
3. Cultivate a Mindful Presence: Practice mindfulness to enhance your presence in the moment. Being fully present allows you to notice and appreciate the wonders around you, whether in nature, art, or daily life.
4. Share Wonder with Others: Share wonder with others. Invite friends or family to join you in activities that evoke a sense of awe. Sharing these experiences can deepen connections and create lasting memories.

Benefits of Cultivating Wonder:

1. Positive Emotional Impact: Experiencing wonder has a positive emotional impact. It can evoke feelings of joy, inspiration, and amazement, contributing to overall emotional well-being.
2. Encourages Lifelong Learning: Wonder fosters a love for learning. Individuals who regularly engage in activities that evoke awe are more likely to be curious and motivated to explore new ideas and concepts throughout their lives.
3. Strengthens Resilience: Cultivating wonder strengthens resilience. Awe-inspiring experiences can provide a source of inspiration and motivation during challenging times, fostering a resilient mindset.
4. Deepens Connection with the World: Wonder deepens the connection with the world. It encourages individuals to see

beauty and fascination in the ordinary, fostering a sense of connectedness to the environment and the people around them.

Adapt to Your Preferences:

1. Personalize Wonder-Inducing Activities: Personalize wonder-inducing activities based on your preferences. Tailor experiences to align with your interests, whether it's exploring scientific wonders, artistic creations, or natural landscapes.

2. Incorporate Wonder into Daily Life: Incorporate wonder into your daily life. Cultivate a mindset that appreciates the small moments of beauty and awe in routine activities, such as watching a sunrise, listening to music, or observing the details of nature.

3. Create a Wonder Jar: Create a wonder jar where you can deposit notes or symbols representing moments of wonder. Regularly revisit the jar to relive and appreciate these experiences, fostering a continuous sense of awe.

4. Join Wonder Communities: Join communities or groups that share a passion for wonder. Engaging with others who appreciate and actively seek awe-inspiring experiences can enhance your own sense of wonder and provide opportunities for shared exploration.

Regularly engaging in activities that evoke a sense of wonder is a transformative tool that enhances overall well-being, promotes curiosity, and fosters a deeper connection with the world. By intentionally seeking awe-inspiring moments, individuals can cultivate a mindset that appreciates the beauty and marvels present in everyday life.

75) Practice Mindful Consumption:

Anecdote: Picture a mindful meal. Consuming consciously extends to all aspects of life.

Interpretation: Be intentional in what you consume, whether it's food, media, or material possessions.

Practical Tool: Pause to consider the impact and necessity of what you consume, making mindful choices aligned with your values. The practical tool encourages individuals to pause and consider the impact and necessity of what they consume, making mindful choices aligned with their values. This approach emphasizes the importance of conscious and intentional decision-making when it comes to consumption, taking into account ethical, environmental, and personal considerations.

Pause and Consider Consumption Impact:

1. Reflect on Values: Take time to reflect on your values. Consider what matters most to you, including ethical considerations, environmental sustainability, and personal well-being. This reflection provides a foundation for making mindful choices aligned with your principles.

2. Assess Necessity: Before making a purchase or consuming a product, assess its necessity. Ask yourself whether the item or experience adds value to your life and aligns with your priorities. This step helps in avoiding impulsive or unnecessary consumption.

3. Environmental Impact: Consider the environmental impact of what you consume. Evaluate the production processes, sourcing,

and potential waste associated with a product or service. Opt for choices that minimize harm to the environment and support sustainable practices.

4. Ethical Considerations: Examine the ethical considerations related to your consumption choices. Research the ethical practices of companies, brands, or services you support. Make choices that align with your values and contribute to ethical business practices.

Why Mindful Consumption Matters:

1. Reduces Environmental Footprint: Mindful consumption reduces your environmental footprint. By making choices that prioritize sustainability and ethical practices, you contribute to a more environmentally conscious and responsible lifestyle.

2. Aligns with Personal Values: Making mindful consumption choices aligns with your personal values. It ensures that your actions are in harmony with your beliefs, fostering a sense of integrity and purpose in your lifestyle.

3. Promotes Responsible Consumerism: Mindful consumption promotes responsible consumerism. By considering the impact of your choices, you contribute to a culture that values conscious decision-making and encourages businesses to adopt more sustainable and ethical practices.

4. Enhances Well-Being: Choosing products and experiences that align with your values can enhance your overall well-being. Mindful consumption fosters a sense of contentment, as your choices are in harmony with your beliefs and contribute to a more fulfilling life.

How to Implement the Tool:

1. Research Products and Brands: Take the time to research products and brands before making a purchase. Look into their ethical practices, environmental policies, and overall impact. Choose brands that align with your values.

2. Practice Minimalism: Embrace minimalism as a lifestyle. Prioritize quality over quantity and focus on experiences that bring genuine joy and value to your life. This approach reduces unnecessary consumption and clutter.

3. Support Local and Sustainable: Support local businesses and products with sustainable practices. Buying locally often reduces the environmental impact associated with transportation, and supporting sustainable practices contributes to a more eco-friendly lifestyle.

4. Mindful Food Choices: Extend mindful consumption to your food choices. Consider the sourcing, production methods, and overall impact of the food you consume. Opt for sustainable and ethically produced food items.

Benefits of Mindful Consumption:

1. Environmental Conservation: Mindful consumption contributes to environmental conservation. Choosing products and services with minimal environmental impact helps preserve natural resources and reduce overall ecological harm.

2. Positive Social Impact: Supporting businesses with ethical practices has a positive social impact. Mindful consumption encourages fair labor practices, responsible sourcing, and community support, contributing to a more equitable society.

3. Financial Wellness: Mindful consumption can lead to financial wellness. By assessing the necessity of purchases and avoiding unnecessary expenses, individuals can save money and allocate resources to experiences or products that truly align with their values.

4. Personal Fulfillment: Making choices aligned with your values enhances personal fulfillment. The satisfaction derived from mindful consumption goes beyond material possessions, fostering a sense of purpose and contentment in your lifestyle.

Adapt to Your Preferences:

1. Customize Your Criteria: Customize the criteria you use to evaluate consumption choices. Your values and priorities are unique, so tailor your considerations to align with what matters most to you, whether it's social responsibility, environmental impact, or other factors.

2. Gradual Changes: Implement mindful consumption gradually. Introduce small changes to your purchasing habits and gradually expand your mindful choices over time. This approach makes the transition more manageable and sustainable.

3. Continuous Reflection: Continuously reflect on your consumption choices. Periodically revisit your values, assess the impact of your choices, and make adjustments as needed. The journey of mindful consumption is ongoing and involves continuous reflection and refinement.

4. Educate Yourself: Stay informed and educate yourself about the impact of different products and industries. Awareness is key to

making informed and mindful choices. Stay curious and seek information to guide your consumption decisions.

Embracing mindful consumption is a transformative tool that empowers individuals to make choices aligned with their values, reduce environmental impact, and contribute to a more ethical and sustainable world. By pausing to consider the impact and necessity of what they consume, individuals can lead more intentional and fulfilling lives.

We've reached the end of our Stoic journey, and I hope these 75 rules have been like little sparks of wisdom in your life.

Remember, Stoicism isn't about becoming a super serious philosopher. It's more like having a set of tools to deal with life's rollercoaster. So, here's a quick recap:

1. You're in Control: Life throws stuff at you, but guess what? You control how you react. Cool, right?

2. What Really Matters: Focus on what's important. Not everything is worth stressing over. Ask yourself, "Is this essential?"

3. Embrace Challenges: Challenges aren't roadblocks; they're detours leading to growth. See them as opportunities, not problems.

4. Enjoy the Journey: Life is short, so own the moment. Find joy in everyday things. Live like you've got bonus time.

5. Be Kind: Spread kindness like confetti. Every person is a chance for a little goodness.

6. Learn, Learn, Learn: Grow a bit every day. Life's a classroom, and every experience is a lesson.

7. Stay Humble: Success or failure, keep your head straight. No need for bragging or despair.

8. Inner Peace: Stillness is key. Find quiet moments; they're like recharging stations for your soul.

So, there you have it. Stoicism isn't a set of strict rules; it's more like a buddy giving you advice on how to make life a bit smoother. Take what works for you, leave what doesn't, and keep on rocking this journey. You've got this!

Incorporating these Stoic principles into daily life can lead to a more resilient, purposeful, and virtuous existence. Remember, the journey toward Stoic wisdom is continuous, and the application of these principles will evolve with practice and reflection.

Embark on a transformative journey with '75 Stoic Rules' – a guide to navigating life's challenges. Each rule is a key to resilience, enriched with stories and practical tips, empowers you to navigate the modern world with timeless wisdom. this book is your key to handling anything life throws your way. Take charge of your journey and make every day a win.

Author: Taha Chaudhary

Some Characters and events in this book are fictitious. Any similarity to real persons, living or dead, is coincidental and not intended by the author.

All rights reserved. No part of this book may be reproduced in any form or by any electronic or mechanical means, including in writing from the publisher, except by reviewers, who may quote brief passages in a review.

Copyright © 2023, Taha Chaudhary

For more books, please visit the above page or visit our website at innersparkgoods.com

Thank You

Printed in Poland
by Amazon Fulfillment
Poland Sp. z o.o., Wrocław
28 May 2024

155a4a04-4575-45f1-9a82-f8f0909f91e6R01